Admiral Rickover and the Nuclear Navy

Hyman George Rickover defied protocol and blasted at conformity and traditional methods to put the United States Navy at the forefront in nuclear propulsion. Honored and known for the contribution he made in engineering the first nuclear-powered submarine, Admiral Rickover was seen in smaller circles as the "prickliest personality in Washington." Heather M. David here records the fascinating story of a "non-conformist in uniform," who armed himself with candor, open criticism, and free thinking in the struggle to convince the government of the need for the development of nuclear power.

LIVES TO

REMEMBER

Admiral Rickover
and the
Nuclear Navy

by HEATHER M. DAVID

G. P. Putnam's Sons
New York

Admiral Rickover
and the
Nuclear Navy

Contents

1

The Adventure

On a balmy evening in June, 1958, at a Navy dock in Seattle, Washington, the nuclear submarine *Nautilus* sat motionless in the water. Aboard, her crew went about their routine duties and conversed cheerfully about their impending trip across the Atlantic to the warm climate of Panama, where they would be rewarded for the long undersea voyage with some time in the sun.

But even as they chatted in the crews' mess, two dark figures scuttled surreptitiously aboard the submarine. One of the officers greeted them with whispered instructions, motioning them down below to a wardroom away from where the crew was gathering.

Satisfied they were unobserved, the two locked themselves in and waited for the submarine to embark.

In the captain's quarters, Commander William R.

Anderson studied some documents. In one hand he had a set of orders marked CONFIDENTIAL which told him to proceed submerged to Panama. In the other, he held a TOP SECRET document which instructed the *Nautilus* to Portland, England.

Now Portland, England, was not an unusual destination, nor one which normally would have required any secrecy. But the bombshell was the route the submarine would take—"by way of the North Pole."

The need for extreme security was great. Such a route, the U.S. Navy knew full well, would take the submarine through the Bering Strait, far from the territorial waters claimed by the Soviet Union but potentially near some of her naval operations off the coast.

In the second place, the Navy felt it had stubbed its toe badly in the eyes of the world when it had attempted to launch an artificial earth satellite the previous fall with a Vanguard rocket.

The failure of the Vanguard on the launching pad could not have been more poorly timed, coming just after the successful Soviet Sputnik satellite launches.

Unfortunately, the Vanguard fiasco occurred with the attention of the world focused upon it. The Defense Department wanted no repetition of its embarrassment if the *Nautilus'* dangerous mission did not succeed.

The crew may have got some hint that something unusual was happening earlier that day, when a spare, wiry admiral was seen poking around the *Nautilus*, carefully checking over every inch of the nuclear reactor power plant. He was Admiral Hyman George

Rickover, creator, originator, instigator, and chief advocate and conscience of the nuclear submarine program. Commander Anderson treated him with deference and attentiveness, for the admiral could ask a mean question and was known for his uncanny ability to ferret out any problems.

If there were bugs in the power plant, this wiry little man with the intense, probing eyes would find them. But after two hours of careful examination, he pronounced the reactor fit for the voyage.

The *Nautilus* was not completely new to the polar region. In August of 1957 she had first started out to achieve what another *Nautilus* had failed to do. In 1931, a polar excursion had been attempted by Sir Hubert Wilkins. But the brave Englishman's efforts ended when his *Nautilus*, a boat literally salvaged from the scrap pile, lost its diving fins and its machinery became frosted over.

The latter-day *Nautilus,* the world's first nuclear submarine, was accompanied on her initial voyage by a conventional submarine, the *Trigger,* which waited patiently beside the ice pack as the *Nautilus* made forays under the gray-white blanket. During this voyage the nuclear submarine proved eloquently that she no longer was second fiddle to the conventional sub.

This first excursion had set records. During that August, 1957, the submarine traveled 150 miles under the ice cap, farther than any known man-made vessel. Unlike Wilkins' sub, which he hoped would be able to skip from break to break in the ice for gulps of air, the *Nautilus* could stay submerged indefinitely.

As a matter of fact, as the *Nautilus* made her way deeper into the polar region, it became obvious that Wilkins' idea never would have been successful; the few lakes and ice breaks were too far apart for a conventional submarine to look for respite from the airless underwater.

The *Nautilus* had run into some difficulties during that 1957 trip, losing one of her periscopes on a loose ice block and badly damaging the other. But her biggest problem was trying to achieve accurate navigation. Although Commander Anderson's orders would have permitted a try at the Pole, at 86 degrees latitude gyroscope problems brought the voyage to a halt. Fear of becoming hopelessly lost prompted the skipper to order a retreat, and the boat returned south to other duties.

The idea of attempting the actual polar crossing had germinated with that trip. Secret meetings were held in Washington at the White House, the Navy Department, and the Pentagon. Commander Anderson was asked to give his view on whether such a feat was possible.

It would be no small task. The Arctic waters were roughly charted, and inaccurately for the most part. The ice which was swept by snow and wind and changing weather was a constantly shifting element impossible to predict. While most ships have only three fronts to worry about—two sides and the depth of the water below, the submarine would have a fourth—the thickness of the ice above.

There was at least one known danger area in the Bering Strait and the Chukchi Sea, through which the sub would have to navigate to get to the Arctic

Ocean. Here the ice was thick and jagged, and the water extremely shallow for comfortable submarine operations. The question was: Could the boat find a tunnel between the ice and the shallow bottom? If she were punctured by a jagged ice floe, would the crew be trapped under the ice, miles from the nearest airhole?

Despite these frightening considerations, the decision was made to give it a try. New high-power sonar and other electronic gear was secretly fitted into the vessel. One extremely important addition was an inertial navigation system, which would measure each movement of the vessel in relation to the earth and compute its exact location at all times. At the North Pole, where compasses would run wild in the magnetic field, this was a necessity.

To keep the real truth out of the papers, cover stories were made up to tell the press about the *Nautilus'* activities. *Nautilus* was going on an extended tour with "ice" operations, the Navy said blandly, thus accounting for the winter clothing and antifreeze being loaded aboard.

Just before the intended departure, Commander Anderson and the Navy's top Arctic expert, Dr. Waldo Lyon, took a commercial airliner from Seattle to Alaska in preparation for a reconnaissance of the polar area. Anderson wore civilian clothes and had an assumed identification card made up to avoid tipping anyone off to the interest of the *Nautilus'* skipper in the North Pole. Chartering a bush pilot's aircraft in Alaska, they flew over the area, noting the size of the ice floes and mapping the most likely-looking routes.

Even on the evening of the departure, the crew was

not told of its final destination. Secrecy was observed to the hilt, and Anderson ordered the *Nautilus'* telltale identification numbers on the sail to be painted over. Since it had been announced that the *Nautilus* was en route to Panama, no one would now be able to identify her and question her presence should she be spotted steaming northward.

At last, as the *Nautilus* cast off, Anderson divulged the boat's true destination to the crew. Their reaction was one of excitement and anticipation. The two men who had slipped aboard that last night—Dr. Waldo Lyon and an assistant—were introduced to the crew members and released from their locked hiding place. The two had been hidden, it was explained, because Dr. Lyon was well known as the Navy's Arctic expert. His presence on board the *Nautilus* would immediately have tipped off curious onlookers as to the boat's destination.

The *Nautilus* slipped quickly beneath the waves and the voyage began. The crew set about carefully checking all the ice-detection gear and calibrating and recalibrating the sonar and navigation equipment. On Friday, the thirteenth of June, the boat started to enter the Bering Strait. But as the *Nautilus* moved closer to its destination, the ice floes grew ominously larger. After trying several routes, the skipper found himself only more perilously closed in by the deadly ice. Regretfully, he radioed his decision to retreat to the Chief of Naval Operations, Admiral Arleigh Burke, who was one of the few men even in Washington who knew about the secret mission.

After a brief stay at Pearl Harbor in the Hawaiian Islands, Commander Anderson ordered the *Nautilus* under way once more. Again, great secrecy was observed. At one point as the *Nautilus* neared the Siberian area, another vessel was sighted. It was determined immediately that it was not an American ship, and the *Nautilus* slunk lower into the sea to avoid detection.

The shallow Chukchi Sea, which had proven to be impassable before, was far less forbidding this time. Much of the huge jagged ice pack had melted, and the boat edged across without incident.

But the polar ice cap itself was an awesome sight. Great ragged ice mountains rose into the air from the surface, with their roots hidden deep in the water. Some of them projected as far as 75 feet downward from the surface.

The sonar recording pen traced the outline of the ice ceiling above, the line jumping up and down the page in the weird shapes of nature's architecture. With their hearts practically in their mouths, the officers of the *Nautilus* watched the pen scratch out a pattern perilously close to the line which marked the course of the submarine.

The goal was near. Now completely depending upon the inertial navigation system, it was calculated that the *Nautilus* was only four-tenths of a mile from the North Pole. Commander Anderson called a moment of silence for prayers of thanks, for peace, and in honor of the brave explorers who had been that way before.

After a brief countdown, the moment at last arrived. On August 3, 1958, the *Nautilus* made history. The navigator recorded the news, filling out his position log "U.S.S. *Nautilus*, latitude 90 degrees north, longitude, indefinite. Distance to the North Pole, zero."

When at last the news was announced to the world, America was jubilant. The nuclear submarine had captured a "first" in history of tremendous impact and importance, and with it some of the national prestige lost when the Soviet Sputnik first beeped its way around the globe.

As soon as the *Nautilus* moved southward, a helicopter was dispatched to fetch Commander Anderson to Washington for honors at the White House. There President Dwight D. Eisenhower conferred the first Presidential Unit Citation to be awarded in peacetime to Anderson on behalf of the *Nautilus* crew. Anderson himself was given high honors.

Forgotten, or perhaps excluded, in the excitement was the spare little man who had given the *Nautilus* reactor her final check that fateful day in June. Far from being the Hollywood kind of hero press agents dream about and the military likes to parade, the quizzical, perfection-seeking admiral often provoked more frustration than adulation in Naval circles.

But the *Nautilus'* moment did not belong to her crew alone, and Commander Anderson full well knew this. Characteristically, it took some arguments to do it, but at long last Admiral Hyman G. Rickover was given his due. When the *Nautilus* steamed into the New York harbor for a hero's welcome, the President's own representative was just a bookish-looking engineer, but he was the man who truly could be called the Father of the Nuclear Submarine.

2

Early Beginnings

Hyman Rickover, the man who would one day become the driving force behind as yet undreamed of developments in nuclear technology, was born in Russian Poland on January 27, 1900. Life in that area was hard indeed, and the aspiration of many Jewish fathers was to take their families to other countries— often America, when they could. The elder Rickover, Abraham, was one of these. A Jewish tailor, he managed to save 100 rubles or about $50, and thus made his way to America.

In 1904, two years after he set up his tailor shop in New York's East Side, he was able to send for his family, which then consisted of Ruchal, his wife; Fanny, who was eight, and Hyman. The small troupe made its way across Germany until it reached Antwerp, staying with Jewish families along the way. At Antwerp, the children got their first view of large

17

oceangoing ships. Fanny was quoted later as saying that her brother burst into tears at the sight and sound of the huge vessels.

In 1910, Abraham moved his growing family from the crowded East Side to Chicago, two years after the birth of another daughter, Gitel. Here they settled in suburban Lawnsdale, where Abraham's tailor business flourished in a modest fashion. By 1919 he was able to set up a small garment factory, which would keep operating for many years afterward.

Despite the promise of solvency in the tailoring business, money was not plentiful in the Rickover family. Young Hyman knew the meaning of hard work early. To help supplement the family income, he worked at a number of odd jobs, including delivery boy and Western Union messenger. These duties required manning his bicycle from three o'clock each afternoon until eleven at night. While he was considered an earnest and bookish boy, his marks, understandably enough, were not outstanding. One year, he was forced to attend summer school to make up failing grades in two subjects to which he did not have time to devote enough attention. His social life also was by necessity almost nonexistent, with neither leisure nor money to devote to the sports events or parties enjoyed by his classmates.

When it came time to think about college, it was clear that there would be no extra funds to support such a luxury. Young Rickover's only hope was to win a scholarship—a hope which did not appear too bright in the light of his scholastic record.

Through friends, the plight of the hard-working

boy was brought to the attention of Chicago's Congressman, Adolph Sabath. In 1918, Rickover received a much-coveted appointment to the United States Naval Academy. This first evidence of the power of politics must have impressed young Rickover with all that it could bring about; Congress certainly became his most influential and receptive ally in future years.

To gain admission to the academy, it was still necessary to pass a stiff entrance exam. With his lifetime savings in hand, Rickover said good-bye to his family to quarter himself near the academy to prepare. First trying a special prep school attended by other aspirants to the academy, then characteristically setting out on his own program of study, he crammed successfully.

At the academy he continued to follow the lonely path which seemed to be his destiny. The mystique of the athletic team, the military field, the camaraderie among the midshipmen, eluded him as he passed the four years studying quietly in his room.

He was graduated in 1922 in the top quarter of his class by virtue of his scholarship, his marks in military drill and the like contributing little to the class average. These phrases were included in the notation in his yearbook: "Neither a star on the gridiron nor a terror in the pool, yet did he loom large through the chalk screens. He is a thorough Englishman with regard to humor, appreciating only Spanish jokes." Nevertheless, in spite of his failure to fit the mold at the academy, Rickover decided to have a go at a Navy career.

The first assignment given the young ensign was to the destroyer U.S.S. *La Vallette*, which was cruising leisurely on the West Coast. He traveled to join her on the Navy transport *Argonne*, getting a look at the Panama Canal on the way. Upon reaching the coast, he temporarily was assigned to the destroyer *Percival*, where, it is related, he faced his first crisis.

As temporary duty officer substituting for an absent officer, Rickover was in charge of the ship when a small explosion occurred below, and one man was badly injured. While the man obviously needed medical attention, none of the *Percival's* boats was alongside to take the man to a doctor.

Flashing a nearby ship, Rickover requested that it send a doctor. Then a seemingly ridiculous argument developed over Navy protocol, which says that junior ships by tradition must send boats to senior ships. After several rounds of messages, Rickover conveyed the idea that he had no boat to send and that the man was seriously injured. In spite of hallowed traditions, the senior ship would have to send its own boat. This kind of incident was not calculated to instill reverence for Navy tradition in harassed junior officers.

The young officer finally reached the *La Vallette*, and his record was good for the two years he spent there. Typically, he studied until he was expert in the workings of the ship and pointed out inefficient practices and waste when he saw it. His initiative apparently impressed the captain of the ship, who promoted him to engineering officer, a high position for a relative greenhorn.

He carried excellent reports with him to the battleship U.S.S. *Nevada,* his next tour of duty. Here he was immediately assigned to the engineering department, where he tackled a new set of challenges with enthusiasm, poring over wiring diagrams and schematics until he began to know the workings of the ship. His interest and ability to learn and make improvements won him the position of electrical officer. Only three years out of the Naval Academy, he innovated a 500-unit battle telephone system which revolutionized communications on the ship.

On the *Nevada,* it is reported, Rickover's ingenuity and unorthodox approach struck a chord with the captain, C. S. Kempff, an intelligent and forward-thinking man. This rapport and his hard work resulted in a promotion to lieutenant, junior grade.

A favorite story related by Rickover's admirers originated in this period, and it runs like this: The young officer, to whom sociabilities were of the lowest order of importance, was directed by the captain to attend a reception for an admiral on a nearby flagship and to appear in his proper lieutenant junior grade rank. After hastily getting a new half-stripe sewed on the sleeves of his uniform, he boarded a launch. However, as he got off the boat onto the flagship, he left a discreet order.

Making his way through the crowd of celebrants, he paid the courtesies of the receiving line, shook the admiral's hand, and kept on moving. Almost without pause, he made a beeline for the other side of the ship, zipped down the ladder, and stepped back into the launch, which had pulled around to meet him to convey him posthaste back to his own ship and his electrical work.

After a pleasant tour on the *Nevada,* Rickover, now five years out of the academy, became eligible and applied for graduate work at Annapolis. There he elected to further his knowledge in electrical engineering. Now he could find answers to some of the technical questions which had puzzled him. And he must have begun to see how new theories in engineering and technology could be used to streamline a Navy going soft and lazy in the peacetime lull.

In 1929, Rickover was sent to Columbia University as part of his graduate work, entering the engineering school. Here were libraries, excellent professors, and an intellectual atmosphere relatively undisturbed by the events taking place on Wall Street and in the international financial world at that time. He stayed at the International House, along with a number of foreign students furthering their education in various graduate fields.

Here, more than any other school he had attended, he was accepted and admired for what he could add to the frequent bull sessions the students held on topics of the day.

It was at one of these sessions—prophetically one in which Rickover delivered an impassioned speech on the need for some fifteen cruisers which were in danger of being cut by Congress out of the Navy's budget—that Rickover met a young graduate student who was studying international law. This girl, Ruth D. Masters, soon became his companion on long walks and on visits to libraries and shows, and in 1931 they were married.

Upon receiving a master's degree in electrical engineering at Columbia, Rickover sought duty on a submarine, with the hopes of getting his own command. Meeting initially with refusal from the Navy Department, a chance meeting with the now Admiral C. S. Kempff, his former *Nevada* captain, proved to be extremely lucky. Through Kempff's recommendation, Rickover was accepted and dispatched to the Submarine School in New London, Connecticut. Once again he won no popularity honors with his questioning about the training there, but in due time he was graduated.

The first submarine to which Rickover was assigned was designated *S-48* and an unfortunate ship she was. Two other similar subs had recently sunk, and a third sister ship had had a severe battery explosion, the greatest fear of the submariner.

Soon after Rickover's arrival on the *S-48,* when the sub was cruising at sea off the Long Island Sound, smoke was reported in the battery room. As was customary, all men were ordered to assemble on the deck so that they could jump overboard if the battery exploded. While all stood by helplessly, Rickover went below to find that their worst suspicions were indeed true, and the acid-filled battery was ablaze. With no real knowledge of how to deal with the situation, he instinctively reached for blankets to smother the blaze, and no doubt saved the ship.

Rickover received a Navy citation for another feat of bravery which he performed aboard the *S-48.* In this incident, a mess attendant fell overboard at the Coco Solo Submarine Base. The lieutenant jumped overboard and held his head above water until help arrived, saving him from drowning.

His energies turned to his duties, as engineering officer of the *S-48*, Rickover found much to occupy his time. Overhauling almost all of the mechanical equipment on board, he kept the ship from the Navy yard and in action, even successfully redesigning the electrical-propulsion motors to run more efficiently.

Although Rickover finally was made executive officer, the second in command on the ship, he disappointingly was not given his own command. Again, perhaps, his "loner" personality stood in his way. As in the past, he spent his time in his quarters, forsaking the noisy shore leaves enjoyed by the other men. He continued his self-improvement program with Naval War College correspondence courses, even including one on international law so that he could converse more expertly with his new wife, who had obtained her PhD in this field.

Some ten years into his Navy career, Rickover was given a job in the office of the inspector of Naval materiel in Philadelphia, Pennsylvania. Although perhaps not the most challenging job in the Navy, he set about to get the most out of it that he could, improving equipment and learning about the methods of the industrial suppliers with whom he dealt. A particular interest was in submarine storage batteries, which would lead to new thoughts about submarine power and propulsion at a later date.

In 1934, he joined the battleship U.S.S. *New*

Mexico as assistant engineering officer. Here he made a name for himself for his economy drives, bringing to the ship the honor of being first in the fleet in fuel conservation, but little personal popularity to himself among the crew, some of whom wore overcoats to press home their point that his penny-pinching was making them cold.

Rickover's first command was the U.S.S. *Finch*, a minesweeper which he was to pick up in China in 1937. To his dismay, he found the vessel in terrible condition, rusty and dirty. To add to the ignominy, it turned out that the *Finch*'s main mission was to tow gunnery targets out to sea for the bigger ships' target practice. The crew's morale was extremely low.

The new captain immediately took steps to impose strong discipline and to attempt to put the *Finch* into shape worthy of the U.S. Navy. Soon, patches of red lead covered the rust spots, and its machinery was oiled and overhauled. When Japan began its invasion of China in 1937, the *Finch* was one of the U.S. vessels used in the evacuation of Americans and British from Shanghai. The polka-dotted vessel was a thankful sight to the anxious refugees as it steamed down the Whangpoo River. Yet the command was not exactly the career dreamed about by midshipmen at the Naval Academy.

Later that year, Rickover began a new career. Now having passed the fifteen-year service mark in the Navy, he became eligible for and applied to become an "engineering duty only" officer. This category would take him out of the line of ship commands but more into the line of work for which his education fitted him. At the end of the year, he was ordered to report to Cavite, in the Philippines. There he became the assistant planning officer of the Navy yard, where he was to stay for two years.

The imprint of Rickover's personality on the Navy yard was soon as obvious as it was on almost everything with which he was associated. The word soon spread that Cavite was "a tough place to get into." Each repair order had to be thoroughly backed and justified and cause shown why the job could not be done by the ship's own engineering department. Inefficiency and waste, as always, were his mortal enemies, and he had no patience for those who would condone them.

At last, in 1939, Rickover was summoned to Washington to assume the post of second in command in the Naval Bureau of Ships Electrical Section. It can be safely assumed that none of the Navy hierarchy dreamed of what they were bringing down upon themselves when they called on the spare little man. Although he had a good record in engineering and bookkeeping matters, he had yet shown no propensity toward becoming a great naval officer or innovator.

The increase of hostilities by the Japanese and Germans throughout the world led the Navy to strengthen its sea forces, calling up experienced officers from shore-bound posts. The chief of the small electrical section was one of these, and his deputy, Hyman Rickover, automatically moved into his place as head of the 200-strong group. By no means just carrying on in the pattern of his predecessor, the new chief set out to strengthen the group, recruiting promising engineers wherever he could find them.

It was not the kind of job in which most Navy men would see any attraction, for it was concerned with electrical circuitry, batteries, fuse boxes, and other such unglamorous equipment. But here there was challenge. There was sport a-plenty in tackling some of the seemingly impossible jobs and satisfaction in cutting through the traditional, unworkable ways of doing things, straight to the heart of the problem to devise a solution.

3

Under the Sea

The first vessel to carry a man below the surface of the sea, history tells us, was the glass barrel which carried Alexander the Great into the depths of the Mediterranean Sea some 2,300 years ago. Alexander also is credited with pioneering in the field of undersea warfare, having commissioned some of his men—at least the better swimmers among them—to attack ships from their undersides while breathing through rudimentary snorkels.

The principle of displacement was worked out by a Greek who lived a century after Alexander, around 200 B.C. Archimedes determined that a floating object actually must be affected by a force pushing upward against it. This force which supported the boat, he said, must be equal to the weight of the water which has been pushed aside by the object settling on the water. Displacement thus is the weight of the water the hull of a vessel displaces as it rests on the water.

For an object to change its depth in the water, it must be able to change its weight, like a fish which can inflate and deflate air bladders as it swims from the surface to the depths of the sea. Submarines also work on this principle, allowing compressed air to expand into a tank to rise to the surface, expelling this air to dive.

Leonardo da Vinci, the Italian genius of the Renaissance who dreamed of airplanes and other modern miracles, also conceived the idea of a vessel which would travel under the water. Fearing the effects such an invention would have on warfare, he hid his plans.

Inventions were not the entire property of the Italians and Greeks, however, for an Englishman named William Bourne actually published a design for a submersible boat in his *Inventions and Devises* in 1578. This boat, to be contrived of wood and leather, was to be submerged by a crew using hand vises to contract the sides of the boat, reducing its volume and thus its displacement. A huge hollow mast would project to the surface, bringing air to the crew. However, Bourne never got his project beyond the paper design stage, so no one knows whether he could have actually made it work, although it is doubtful.

Others also planned and dreamed, but the first underwater boat was not built until the same year the *Mayflower* sailed to the New World. Dr. Cornelius Van Drebbel, a Dutchman, was able to convince England's King James to give him funds to build three of his boats. These boats, also made of wood with heavy coverings of greased leather and powered by a dozen rowers, made their cumbersome way to depths of 12 to 15 feet in the Thames River. It is even reported that King James himself may have been a passenger in one of these vessels. Drebbel also is credited with another first. It is believed quite possible that he discovered the art of compressing oxygen into containers for use in replenishing the air in his submarine.

A century later, in 1747, the forerunner of modern submarines' ballast tanks appeared on a vessel built by a man named Symons who also operated in the Thames River. Symons' craft had a number of leather bottles built into the hull, which could be filled with water to submerge or have the water squeezed out to rise again to the surface.

These rudimentary attempts were followed by further work by the unfortunate John Day, an Englishman who became submarinedom's first victim. Day, on June 28, 1774, sank to the bottom of Plymouth Harbor, where the intense pressure of the water at that record depth—some 132 feet—collapsed the walls of his ship before he could release the ballast and rise to safety.

Two years later, however, the submarine was first used as a weapon of war when David Bushnell made his historic attack on the British warship *Eagle* in the New York harbor with his submersible boat, the *Turtle*.

The *Turtle,* so named because it resembled two turtle shells joined together, was large enough only for one man. Various accounts give its speed, which came from hand propulsion by the lone crew member, as from one to three knots per hour. It had a 30-minute stay time at depth, which Bushnell calculated with a unique depth gauge of his own invention.

The weapon was a 150-pound cask of gunpowder activated by a time fuse. The pilot of the *Turtle* was to approach the enemy ship underwater, bore a wooden screw into the British ship, and attach a line leading to the cask. On September 6, 1776, Sergeant Ezra Lee of the Continental Army attempted to carry out this plan but found to his intense dismay that the H.M.S. *Eagle* had a copper bottom. Bushnell tried again during the War of 1812, but this attempt ended in like failure.

Yet in spite of an apparent lack of success, Bushnell had made a point. No longer could ships cruise heedlessly, their nether parts unguarded.

One of the men who was impressed by Bushnell's idea was Robert Fulton, peripatetic inventor of a number of things. Although he would later gain fame for his design of the steamboat, much of Fulton's mature life was spent in trying to get support for his idea on the submarine. Making a meager living by painting, Fulton canvassed the kingdoms of the day until in 1800 he finally persuaded Napoleon Bonaparte to finance his submarine, the *Nautilus.*

The first *Nautilus,* so named for the shellfish whose sail it resembled, had a metal hull and was propeller-driven but man-powered. One of its innovations was a horizontal rudder, precursor to the diving plane.

Flasks of compressed air permitted a sustained dive, and the *Nautilus* was able to submerge for five hours.

Fulton actually blew up two ships—one British and one French—in his attempt to attract money from either of these countries. But after losing Napoleon's backing he never was able to get a major commitment from any country, and he returned to America to die in 1815 without having convinced anyone that the submarine was a completely practical idea.

It was not until the Civil War that the first really successful offensive attack was made by a submarine on a surface ship. On February 17, 1864, the Confederate submersible *Hunley* sank the U.S.S. *Housatonic,* a corvette in Charleston Harbor. Manpower, however, still was the mode of the day, and would be for the next thirty years.

In 1886 another *Nautilus* made submarine history. This was a vessel built by the English which had two 50-horsepower electric motors operated by a storage battery. This method of underwater propulsion would span the next sixty years, although surface propulsion for submarines would be uprated in the United States in 1912 with the use of diesel-electric engines.

Those who still took submarines lightly got a rude awakening when on September 22, 1914, a German Unterseeboot, *U-9*, sank three British light cruisers off the Belgian coast in less than half an hour. More than 1,200 officers and men were lost in the sinking of the three vessels, while *U-9* slunk away unscathed. The feat was followed by a number of successful kills for the 28-vessel oceangoing German submarine force, including the inflammatory sinking of the British passenger liner the *Lusitania*.

All told, about 5,500 merchant ships and fishing vessels were lost to German U-boats, bringing the United States into the war in April, 1917. By contrast, fewer than 200 U-boats were lost in combat. Yet, the Allies greatly developed antisubmarine warfare skills, devising such equipment as underwater listening devices which would lead to sonar detection techniques.

During the Second World War, faced with the invention of radar which relentlessly sought out the German submarine on the surface at night, the Germans added snorkel gear, permitting operation of the diesel engine below the surface by virtue of the air it brought down and the exhaust it returned to the surface. Yet the snorkel had one fault, and that was that it left a wake clearly marking the path of the submerged vessel for enemy trackers.

The United States launched its first fleet submarine in 1936 and mass-produced it in World War II. American submarines, by no means as many in number as the German force, were of tremendous importance in the defeat of Japan. They sank more than 5,500,000 tons of Japanese cargo ships and fighting vessels, accounting for 63 percent of the total. While the submarines also sank more than 200 Japanese naval vessels, it was the crippling of her supply lines of rubber and oil from the East Indies that had the most profound effect.

The most significant advances in submarine technology, however, were in the detection instruments used to hunt them down. During World War I, the problem of locating the dread German U-boats was so overwhelming that one group of officers even seriously considered using sea gulls and seals. The theory was that if sea gulls could be trained to perch on submarine periscopes, where they would be led to believe that they would find a fish, they would make spotting the periscope much easier. In addition, it was hoped, their tails would hang down, obscuring the view of the conning officer below. But the sea gulls just weren't interested in this project, and all the officers got for their trouble were some high-smelling periscopes. The seals, which it was hoped would follow the submarine, showed the same indifference.

It was the development of radar for aircraft which caught the Germans off guard completely. For many years they had found the fog and dark a sanctuary at night, for they had to spend much of their time on the surface. But with the development of radar by the British, they all too often were greeted, too late to take cover, by the glaring lights of a plane making its bomb run. Although radar had been invented in the late 1930's, it had not been successfully compacted into a size which could feasibly be carried by aircraft until 1942. The Germans countered with a search receiver which indicated that the U-boat was in the radar's beam, but this advantage was short-lived. In 1943, the British introduced an even more advanced radar which was undetectable by the U-boats, and the tide was turned.

Although the snorkel was an improvement which

meant that the submarine could cruise underwater on her diesel engines, her depth was limited by the length of her snorkel. This tube, bringing vital air to the engine and to the crew, was a steel chain to the surface. To dive, and indeed to conduct any of the maneuvers required in combat, the submarine had to revert to its battery-powered electric engine. And these batteries required recharging, a process which consumed eight or nine hours on the surface, or in shallow water just below it, each day.

The submarine with its batteries low was in particular danger, for it had no power to escape, and with a limited amount of torpedo power and its modest deck guns, it was no match for surface ships. Many a deadly cat-and-mouse game was played during the Second World War waiting for a helpless submarine to surface.

The batteries were an ever-present source of danger, as well. While they were being charged, they would give off hydrogen gas, which is highly explosive. A fire in the battery at sea could mean an explosion which would sink the boat and crew. And if the submarine was damaged by a depth charge and seawater entered the batteries, a deadly gas was released.

Thus, while there were improvements in the lot of the submariner and in antisubmarine tactics, the basic principles remained much the same as when Rickover tended to the engineering problems of the *S-48* and probably saved the ship from an explosive battery fire at sea.

Rickover's own crusade during the war, from an office in Washington, was to upgrade the Navy's ships with the best possible electrical equipment in working order. His first attack was on the cataloging system; casting out the bulky, duplicative manuals with which the Navy had been operating, he instructed his hand-picked task force to write its own. But properly organizing and cataloging the Navy's electrical inventory for the first time was by no means enough. He then focused a critical eye on the equipment itself.

He summoned his staff and outlined his plans. This item was not reliable, see that it is, he would say. This should be smaller, no reason for all that weight and volume. The Navy should be getting better performance for its money on this one—beef up the design and see that it does. He tackled industry, fearlessly shouting orders to salesmen and company presidents themselves. His tactics were greeted with resentment and grumbling, but in the end most complied, for they could see that if they wanted future electrical equipment business from the Navy, they'd have to cooperate. There was no getting around him.

Naval electric gear became far more reliable and battleworthy under the fine hand of the chief of the electrical section, and his name became known as one who could get a tough and complicated job done. But he left a number of squelched toes in his path, and some of his unorthodox methods shook Navy traditionalists to the boots.

One almost unbelievable incident, reported by Clay Blair, Jr., in his book *The Atomic Submarine,* is a case in which Rickover on his own arranged a contract of from $8,000,000 to $12,000,000 with General Motors without Navy approval.

According to Blair, it happened when the captain learned about the heavy damage being done to British naval vessels by the secret German magnetic mine. Confronted by the fact that the Navy's Bureau of Ordnance had no plans for a counterweapon, Rickover decided he would have to devise one himself. After studying British reports on what they were attempting to do to sweep the mines, he arranged to get a sample of the electric cable which the British were counting on to explode the mines. Rickover analyzed the cable and had plans drawn for a generator to provide the electric current. At this point, he did present his plan to his superior Naval officers, but he met with indifference. However, this apparently did not bother him in the least.

First he started a cable company on the manufacture of the secret cable, overlooking patent infringements all the while. Then he got General Motors, who had no inkling that Rickover might not be authorized to initiate the project, to begin work on a diesel-powered generator to charge the cable. The company, under the understanding that it was a top-priority wartime project, made it top secret and expedited the assembly of materials and components.

Someone in the Navy's purchasing department began to put two and two together and alerted Navy brass to the situation. Rickover had, on his own authority only, made an unofficial contract for millions of dollars with a leading American corporation. The formal contract, still unsigned, was lying unnoticed in red tape in the Bureau of Supplies and Accounts.

When the admirals called Rickover on the carpet for an explanation, he told them earnestly that he was trying only to rush through equipment vitally needed by the fleet. Luckily, top officials at the Bureau of Ships appreciated what he had tried to do and formalized the contract immediately. Rickover later was credited with the foresight to push a number of projects important to the Navy.

Perfectionists win admiration but few friends, however, and this was the electrical section chief's lot. His methods of taking matters into his own hands, usurping authority, and going over the heads of those who got in his way made him disliked in many Navy circles. All this would catch up with him later. Yet, for his accomplishments, he was given the Legion of Merit.

Before the end of the war, in 1945, Rickover was sent to Okinawa to take charge of the fleet repair base there. He set out with his usual energy to revamp both personnel and equipment, his wiry figure darting from place to place as he checked his new charge. However, the repair facility was devastated by a typhoon just after the Japanese surrender and ordered closed down by the Navy.

His next assignment was as inspector general of the 19th Mothball Fleet. There, as overseer of the mothballing of the U.S. Navy ships coming off the high seas, his job was to see that machinery was repaired, equipment cleaned and painted and safely put up in a plastic cocoon to protect it from rust and decay in case the ships were needed again in the future. Congress had ordered all military personnel home for separation, however, and the Navy was hard pressed to find able men to do the dirty job.

A better spur could not have been found than in the slight captain, who might be found crawling through the bilges of ships at all hours, pointing out painted-over debris or puddles of water to many a harassed ship captain. As usual, he wrote strongly worded reports on his findings, outlining plans for better utilization of manpower and equipment in all aspects of the task. The job was put on a production-line basis, and Rickover's methods were copied elsewhere. It was to his credit that many of the ships neatly mothballed on the West Coast under his direction were in such good shape that they could be readied in short order when the Korean War broke out six years later.

Meanwhile, there were far-thinking scientists in the Navy who were studying the potential of harnessing nuclear energy to an engine to propel a submarine. Although they had no practical plan for an engine, they realized that the 1938 discovery by the Germans that uranium atoms bombarded with neutrons will split, releasing energy in a process called fission, was extremely significant. Dr. Ross Gunn, chief of the Naval Research Laboratory in Washington, led a group which was studying a number of concepts for submarine propulsion, including hydrogen-peroxide-alcohol steam turbines. The Germans also were secretly working on a hydrogen-peroxide plant for a submarine, led by an innovator named Hellmuth Walter. Yet the hydrogen-peroxide engine did not look promising to Americans until they saw later how far it had been brought by the Germans. And then the United States became committed to another avenue of research.

The big drive was for a method of propulsion which would not require oxygen or air. The group led by Dr. Gunn realized immediately that nuclear energy might provide a solution. In 1939, after consultation with Dr. Enrico Fermi, a plan was proposed to Rear Admiral Harold G. Bowen, chief of the Bureau of Steam Engineering, the parent organization to the Naval Research Laboratory. Two months before Albert Einstein wrote his famous letter to President Franklin D. Roosevelt proposing the use of atomic energy in an explosive bomb, the Navy actually had a report from Dr. Gunn on the use of nuclear propulsion for submarines. Thus it was the Navy which committed the first government money to the study of nuclear fission. Among others, the Carnegie Institution cooperated with the Navy in trying to unlock the secret of nuclear fission, and in January, 1941, one of its chief scientists, Dr. Philip H. Abelson, joined the Naval Research Laboratory to devote full-time effort to it. Abelson and Gunn did work out a method of separating the crucial U-235 uranium isotope, but their work was overshadowed when the Manhattan Engineering District—the atom bomb project—took all priorities in the nuclear field.

Yet in December, 1944, a governmental committee

studying possibilities for the further development and peaceful application of nuclear power urged the initiation of an urgent project: research and development studies to provide power from nuclear sources for the propulsion of naval vessels. The idea also was ventured by Dr. Gunn in testimony before a Congressional Committee on Atomic Energy.

There were many in the Navy who feared and opposed the idea of further work on atom power, and with good reason. The awful destructive power of the bomb threatened to make naval power ineffective. On July 3, 1946, about fifty ships no longer needed by the Navy were ordered to a lagoon off the atoll of Bikini in a Pacific archipelago 250 miles south of Kwajalein.

The ships, including submarines, destroyers, heavy cruisers, and a carrier, bore a most unusual crew. This included almost 200 tethered goats, 150 pigs, thousands of caged rats, and hundreds and hundreds of instruments. These modern day Noah's Arks were anchored in a circle five miles across to be sacrificed for a better understanding of the atom bomb explosion in Operation Crossroads.

Two atomic bombs already had made their point at Hiroshima and Nagasaki. Now the Navy wanted precise measurements of their destructive potential on the sea. To get them, it would conduct the world's largest experiment in ordnance and physics.

The human crews were taken off the valiant old vessels, among them such names as the *Skate*, the *Nevada,* the *Arkansas*, and the *Independence*. A lone B-29 out of Kwajalein approached from the south, carrying a Nagasaki-type atomic bomb in its belly. Some ten miles away, aboard special ships, the experiment's observers watched the bomb burst hit the silent fleet, releasing thousands of tons of explosive power in one giant burst. A mammoth cloud roared skyward, the shock wave traveling miles. The scene was repeated a few weeks later.

Tests Able and Baker of Operation Crossroads rocked the Navy figuratively as well as literally. More than thirty ships were destroyed, leaving the lagoon strewn with crumpled, twisted, and charred metal which little resembled the once proud fleet.

Yet there were those that protested that the experiments were not realistic, for in real combat that many ships would not have been assembled in such a confined area. Most tried to forget about what they had seen, to take comfort in familiar things in the peacetime task of patrolling the United States' own shores and shipping lanes.

Indeed, many of the scientists who had participated in this great technological and scientific awakening returned to their laboratories, retreating from the awfulness of what they had done. And many others, including leading political and governmental figures, were lulled into a feeling that now that the United States was the sole possessor of the ultimate weapon, all further progress on military equipment could be brought to, if not a standstill, at least a leisurely walk.

Yet a few could look to the future when new weapons and military craft would be needed and were not willing to bask in the peacetime lull. Toward the end of the war, Naval Research Laboratories scientists tried to revive their project on exploratory work on the submarine nuclear reactor. However, the plan was overruled by the Manhattan District, which was concentrating solely on the development of atomic power for explosives. Tremendous secrecy imposed by the District and its chief, General Leslie Groves, on all matters nuclear also thwarted the scientists' attempts to further their research.

Dr. Gunn and a few others were allowed to visit Oak Ridge, where the Manhattan District had its laboratory. Yet, forbidden access to secret data on nuclear fission, the group could accomplish little. When they appealed to Groves, he told them that the only way he could give them access to the information was for them to join the Manhattan District.

The Monsanto Chemical Company, a contractor which operated part of the Oak Ridge Laboratory for the District and which was working on the development of an experimental power pile, was interested in getting other support to further work in providing the United States with practical benefits of the power derived from an atom. It contacted the Army Air Force, the Navy, and a number of industrial firms in the spring of 1946, suggesting that they send representatives to join in a mutual project.

There was some popular support for such a project, and the President himself had publicly stated that the United States would be the benefactor of many improvements to modern living through its development of atomic power.

On March 14, 1946, Secretary of Defense James

Forrestal agreed that military representatives could be sent to Oak Ridge to learn about nuclear fission and to participate in its further development for practical uses.

It was about this time that an energetic little inspector general of the mothball fleet, voraciously reading the news of the day and keeping up with technological developments, made the decision that this was the portent of the future and that he wanted to be involved in it. On one of his trips east, Rickover approached his superiors in the Bureau of Ships and expressed his desire to apply for training in the new science.

The Navy had decided to send eight men to Oak Ridge, headed by a single captain. It first answered Rickover's appeal with a decision to send him to the Massachusetts Institute of Technology for a three-year course in nuclear technology. Another captain was assigned to go to the budding nuclear project in Tennessee.

One of the interesting things about this period is that of the applicants for the Navy nuclear study group, there were no really qualified technical men, except Rickover, who were willing to involve their careers in this new field. In accordance with the prevalent belief that nuclear power was many years in the future, the man chosen as senior officer of the Navy group was a good bureaucrat, who worked well with others. Rickover fell far short of that ideal.

But once again it was one of Rickover's superiors who intervened and set matters to his liking. His Bureau of Ships chief, Admiral Earle Mills, looked

45

over the situation, learned of Rickover's preference, and decided to overrule the previous order, giving him the assignment to Oak Ridge. Rickover's own reaction was to lock himself up with an armload of books on the subject.

When in May, 1946, he reported to Washington for briefings on the assignment, he was given the Navy's files on nuclear energy. Here he ran into the 1939 work by Dr. Gunn and Dr. Abelson. He learned that while these visionaries had even thought about putting atomic energy to work to propel naval vessels, their efforts had been turned toward explosives in support of the Manhattan Project during the war.

Also in the file was the Naval Research Laboratory proposal submitted by its director, Commodore H. A. Schade, for a program of research into nuclear shipbuilding, based upon the work done by Dr. Gunn and his associates.

Yet there was another document which held even more fascination. This was a conceptual plan for a nuclear submarine authored by Dr. Philip Abelson. Abelson suggested that the nuclear power plant use a potassium-sodium alloy as the heat transfer agent between the reactor and the turbine. The reactor would be mounted along the hull of the submarine. The submarine design would use some of the technology developed by the Germans toward the end of the war and revealed in captured plans. However, although designed for very high submerged speeds, the German plan was based on the almost perfected hydrogen-peroxide power plant, not a nuclear reactor.

Abelson estimated that a nuclear submarine capable of operating at 26 to 30 knots submerged for long periods of time without refueling could actually be built by the United States. Within five to ten years, he said, a submarine with perhaps double that speed could be developed. Such a sub, capable of 40 to 60 knots or higher, would use a jet propulsion system in conjunction with its nuclear reactor. Radical modifications of hull design and other features would undoubtedly be needed, requiring an extensive research program, he concluded. Abelson noted that such an undertaking would require high priority and cooperation from the Navy, the Executive Branch, and the Manhattan District, and the Navy would have to have a stronger voice in design and construction of an uranium pile of proper characteristics for the application.

Abelson predicted that operation of the pile would be simple, noting the experience of the Manhattan District. With some amazement, scientists there had recorded how easy it was to control the atomic pile, with operators often doing nothing but recording the instrument readings.

This contrasted sharply with submarine diesel-electric engines, which needed frequent inspections and overhauls. And during the war, the speed of the newest subs was about 21 knots on the surface, but only about 9 knots submerged. Up until now, submarines still were essentially surface vessels.

4

Oak Ridge

Once at Oak Ridge, Rickover involved himself in the operating organization, where he could learn most about what was going on. Although the Monsanto power pile project was not yet under way, he was assigned to the director of operations, from which vantage point he could observe the day-to-day functions of the laboratory and have access to the technical information he wanted to study.

The Monsanto project was known as the Daniels Pile, after Dr. Farrington Daniels, chief scientist in the group. A number of other scientists, industrialists, and military men soon joined the group, among them representatives from the Army Air Force, Westinghouse, General Electric, and other companies. Some industrial concerns were interested in getting involved in the new technology, seeing the possibility of future large equipment contracts from the government. Indeed, a few small contracts already were being let, including some for work on sodium potassium alloys as heat transfer agents from reactors to turbines, as suggested by Dr. Abelson.

General Electric Company also was vitally interested in atomic energy and had contracted to run the plutonium manufacturing installation at Hanford, Washington, for the Manhattan District. GE petitioned for and received funding to build a laboratory near Schenectady, New York, which later became the Knolls Atomic Power Laboratory. GE also saw a great potential market in nuclear energy for naval propulsion and arranged with the Navy, through Admiral Earle Mills, to begin work in its own laboratory on an atomic pile which it hoped would ultimately go into a destroyer.

The other four Naval officers assigned to Oak Ridge were Lieutenant Commander Lou Roddis, Lieutenant Ray Dick, Lieutenant Commander James H. Dunford, and Lieutenant Commander Miles A. Libbey. Roddis was a brilliant engineer who had worked in the Bureau of Ships during World War II. Dick, also an engineer with a particular interest in metallurgy, had come from Ohio State with especially high credentials. The other two were Naval Academy men only six or seven years out of Annapolis.

While the initial understanding was that the Navy group had been assigned to Oak Ridge in a study program, Rickover soon put an end to that. Feeling himself a man with a mission, he put all his energies into a path which would lead to a nuclear submarine. While he had no orders to act as leader of the group, as senior Naval officer he was qualified to fill out the fitness reports the Navy traditionally keeps in each man's record for the duration of his career. These reports have a profound effect on an officer's future command prospects, since they are read by each review board before promotions, so it gave him quite a bit of power over the younger officers, who were soon molded into a Navy team.

The records show that Rickover soon had an organized plan of study for the group, tackling every aspect of interest to Navy purposes. Each week, he submitted a report written by the officers to Washington, under the heading "The Oak Ridge Naval Group."

The Hanford reactors built during the war used uranium metal, which has two isotopes. While the general term "splitting the atom" is used to describe what goes on in a nuclear reactor, it is somewhat misleading, for it does not describe a process like the kinds of conventional "splitting" of wood or some other material. A better term for the process is fission.

The nucleus of the U-235 atom contains 92 protons, or positively charged particles, and 143 uncharged particles called neutrons. These charged and uncharged particles add up to 235. Scientists found that if more neutrons were used to bombard a quantity of uranium, the neutrons would be picked up by the nucleus of the U-235 present. Since this isotope already is somewhat unstable, the addition of more neutrons becomes too much for it and it breaks into two approximately equal large parts, releasing at the same time two or three neutrons along with a tremendous amount of energy. On the average, 2.5 neutrons come out from each fission process. They are minute particles which travel at tremendously high speeds, as much as 30,000,000 feet a second for a distance of about three-ten-thousandths of an inch. At that high speed and in that short distance, they cause a lot of friction, which generates heat. The neutrons released in the process can bombard and split more nuclei in a chain reaction, producing more neutrons to split more U-235 atoms and so on.

For every square centimeter cross section of a reactor core there are 100,000,000,000,000 neutrons that are produced by fission every second of time. For every square inch this amounts to about 6.4 times 10^{14} neutrons every second of time it is operating.

If the process is allowed to go on rapidly and without control, the tremendous amount of energy released creates an enormous explosion; thus the devastating effect of the atom bomb. However, if the reaction is controlled, the energy may be used at will and converted to other usable forms such as steam or electrical energy.

Unfortunately, the U-235 is the least prevalent of the uranium isotopes, accounting for only one out of every 140 atoms of uranium. The most common isotope, U-238, has 146 neutrons and is very stable, meaning that the forces within it are well balanced. It cannot be split by practical means. These heavy atoms absorb neutrons and change into other elements.

Thus, a way must be found to see that the U-235

atoms are increased or get preferential treatment. This can be done by separating the U-235 atoms from the U-238 through diffusion, but this is an expensive process which requires a great quantity of electrical power. Such fuel is called "enriched" uranium.

A reactor which burns only U-235 atoms is called a nonregenerative reactor. It creates waste and eventually depletes the supply of uranium to the point where the waste interferes with the chain reaction.

A more advanced idea which was being studied was the regenerative reactor, which would use natural uranium with both its isotopes present. In it, the neutrons would be allowed to hit the U-238 or heavy atoms, some of which would absorb them. With the first hit, the U-238 atom with the addition of one neutron would weigh 239, becoming a new element called neptunium. After a period of time, one neutron would change to a proton, giving it 93 protons. Somewhat later, another neutron would change to a proton, making a total of 94 protons. It would now be another element, plutonium 239. This element can be removed and purified much more cheaply than can U-235, and can also be used as an atomic fuel.

However, the use of unprocessed uranium was considered impractical for submarines, since it would require carrying huge amounts of the heavy metal. Thus, a design based on an enriched uranium core was conceived.

The neutrons used to bombard the uranium can be fast, slow, or thermal, as the scientists say, or of intermediate speed. The slow ones are best for breaking up U-235. To keep the speeds of these fast-moving particles down to the rate at which they are most effective in producing further fission, a moderator is used. Both hydrogen and graphite are good moderators, thus the use of heavy water, which has double-weight hydrogen or deuterium in some reactors and graphite in others.

There is a certain minimum amount of fuel in a reactor, in its tank of heavy water or core of graphite, which must be present before the reactor will start up or "go critical." The amount of this "critical" mass is determined by a number of things such as the shape of the core, the percentage of enriched uranium in the fuel, the nature of the moderator, and other design factors.

Control rods, usually made of a metal which absorbs neutrons such as boron or hafnium, are used to control the intensity of the chain reaction. The rods can be moved in and out of the reactor core, so that when they are fully inserted, the reactor cannot become critical. As the reactor is started up, the control rods are withdrawn and the chain reaction begins to build up slightly as the neutrons are free to find fissionable material. The rate of the reaction can be held at various levels by adjusting the insertion of the rods.

Some months after they had arrived at Oak Ridge, the Navy group filed a significant report to the Chief of Naval Operations back in Washington. In this document, the men spoke of their conviction that within five to eight years the United States could have a nuclear-powered vessel. With top-level support and funding, the minimum time could even be shaved down, the report said. The letter was circulated in official Washington in the Navy and the Atomic Energy Commission, which was then just being organized out of the Manhattan District.

Meanwhile, the Monsanto power project, the Daniels Pile, was proving to be a disappointing venture. Serious technical problems were daily becoming evident which seemed almost insoluble by the limited work force assigned to the project, and the approach being taken. In addition, there was some question as to the aims of the newly formed AEC. Some felt that it was floundering in disorganization as everyone, scientists, Congress, and the administration, argued over the character of the new organization. Others said that those in it were interested only in making bombs and did not care about the development of means to control and convert nuclear power for other purposes.

The project at General Electric also was disappointing. On a visit to the laboratory at Schenectady, the Navy group found that although the company was pursuing an exciting line of research in a breeder reactor which would produce fissionable material as a side product as it created energy by fission, it seemed more interested in basic research than in the tough task of engineering a reactor for a naval vessel.

The Navy group then turned to a survey of all atomic research in the United States, touring all installations in the field and interviewing the leading scientists. They visited the University of Chicago, where the atom bomb was first conceived in a secret laboratory under a football stadium stand. They toured the AEC's Hanford, Washington, installation, where plutonium for atomic bombs was produced. They talked to scientists at E. O. Lawrence's radiation laboratory at the University of California, Berkeley, and at the Los Alamos Scientific Laboratory run by the AEC in New Mexico.

They impressed at least one scientist during this trip. Dr. Edward Teller, the bushy-browed scientist who had worked on the first atomic bomb and who would later become known as the Father of the Hydrogen Bomb, was impressed by the knowledge which the group had already picked up on atomic energy developments, as well as by their enthusiasm and enterprise. After hearing the story from Rickover, Teller was prompted to write a letter to those in charge of research and development at the Pentagon.

However, the problems of the Daniels Pile and the direction of the work at GE led top Navy brass to downgrade the potentials for nuclear propulsion developments. With no going project, the possibility seemed far in the future. Thus, the Oak Ridge Navy group led by Rickover was brought back to Washington.

The other Navy officers were assigned to posts elsewhere in the Navy in Washington, and Rickover was given the title of "special assistant" to the chief of the Bureau of Ships for nuclear matters, a post which had little authority and as far as anyone could then see, even less future.

To crown the discouraging situation, the office given the special assistant for nuclear matters was a former ladies' powder room, complete with washbasin on the wall and plumbing on display. But

Rickover had seen enough, and received enough encouragement from nuclear scientists, to know that his idea of a nuclear submarine was attainable. Overlooking the odds, he set about to bring it into reality.

Assessing the little with which he had to work, the captain decided to make the best of it. The Daniels Pile group was fast disintegrating, but there were a few competent scientists and engineers there who were interested in continuing research in nuclear reactors. Rickover made a quiet trip to Oak Ridge and talked to them, spelling out the potential of a smaller reactor capable of being installed in a submarine. They diverted their remaining time to this project.

Rickover's campaign was now directed toward the Navy itself. No research project generated by a military service can live long unless the operational branch of that service—those who must actually use the equipment—says that there is a military requirement for it. If he could obtain such a statement from the Chief of Naval Operations, those who controlled research funds and talent would have to give way.

A letter was drafted through the collaboration of Rickover and Ray Dick, spelling out the need for an atomic-powered submarine. Their hope was that the Chief of Naval Operations, Admiral Chester Nimitz, could be induced to sign the letter, sending it to the Secretary of the Navy.

Then came the task of getting the letter through official channels to Admiral Nimitz. For weeks it made its way from one office to another, hand-carried by those who were in favor of the project, blocked by those who were not. But finally in December, 1947, the letter found its way into the admiral's office and was signed by him.

In essence, this letter was the charter for the nuclear submarine project. It pointed out the strategic and tactical importance of the nuclear submarine and called for an agreement between the Bureau of Ships and the Atomic Energy Commission on a program for design, development, and construction of a nuclear-propulsion plant for a submarine.

The next crucial step was to get a favorable reaction from the Secretary of the Navy. To the little group's gratification, however, he also was convinced of the merit in the idea. The official attitude of the Navy soon underwent a change; this was indeed a powerful ally.

However, Rickover's troop knew that there were two halves to the apple. The project would require a like commitment from the Atomic Energy Commission, without whose cooperation the reactor could never be built. Yet the AEC still floundered in organizational difficulties, with its only forward thrust in the refinement of atomic warheads for weapons. Except for the small group quietly working on the naval reactor, the agency was little interested in such developments.

Yet the Navy knew that the AEC would have to give high priority to the project if it were to succeed. Rickover himself saw the need for a joint organization compiling elements of both organizations under one management, with authority to use fully the facilities of both to undertake the development effort.

It was not until Admiral Mills, chief of the Navy's Bureau of Ships, publicly harpooned the AEC in a scientific meeting on Undersea Warfare in Washington, D.C., that much began to happen. Before an auditorium crowded with top governmental officials and some of the nation's leading scientists, Mills said in no uncertain terms that the AEC had never recognized the submarine power pile as a project, in spite of a widespread impression that such a project was being pushed forward with high priority. Mills made it clear that the AEC was not responding to Navy needs. He also spelled out the importance of the project to the Navy and its belief that the design was technically feasible and almost entirely an engineering problem.

At last the organization was drawn up in the summer of 1948, with Rickover as its head. Wearing two "hats," his Navy captain's hat as the head of the Bureau of Ships Nuclear Power Branch and a civilian hat as the chief of the AEC's Division of Reactor Development Naval Reactors Branch, he mapped out a program.

Within the Navy, engineers began the design of a submarine suitable to house the nuclear reactor. Westinghouse Electric Company was put to work on the design of a heat exchange system for an atomic-power reactor. This system would take the tremendous energy generated by the reactor in the form of heat and work out a method for changing it into power to propel the submarine.

By the end of 1948 Rickover, with his AEC hat on, contracted with Westinghouse for a water-cooled reactor, using enriched uranium as its fuel. The reactor was designated the Submarine Thermal Reactor (STR) because it would operate with neutrons slowed down to moderate speeds, or thermal speeds.

Although there was a long uphill battle against technological and bureaucratic difficulties, a firm foundation had been laid. The seed germinated with health.

Back of the foot-dragging on the part of the Atomic Energy Commission in the 1947-48 period was the universal belief that the United States was the only country in the world having nuclear knowledge. With the tremendous destructive power in its arsenal, the country was complacent in the belief that it had the power to keep the peace indefinitely.

It was scientists in the Naval Research Laboratory who first put an end to this pleasant fantasy. After flying all over the globe to collect samples of rainwater, they tested them for the presence of radioactivity. When they first began the project, they found small amounts of radioactivity from a nuclear test carried by the United States some months before. As time passed, the amount of radioactivity diminished, as could be expected.

But in September, 1949, the count suddenly went up. The scientists called for more samples, and jugs of water began arriving, gathered daily in far outposts in Alaska and the Aleutian Islands. The water was compared with previously taken samples and with water gathered in Washington.

Most scientists and government officials had believed that the Soviets were at least several, and perhaps five or ten, years away from unlocking the secret of nuclear fission. However, unknown to all but their fellow spy-ring members, the secret files of the Atomic Energy Commission at Oak Ridge and other top installations had been infiltrated by spies. Through the work of the Rosenbergs, David Greenglass, and Dr. Klaus Fuchs, much of the basic information which had put the United States in the lead in the nuclear field was known also to the Soviet Union. And that country was sparing nothing to achieve for itself the position of world leadership which then belonged to the United States.

The Soviets had another secret ace concealed in their figurative sleeve. After World War II, the top German rocket experts led by Dr. Wernher von Braun had surrendered to the United States, preferring the Americans to the Russians, with their totalitarian state and their obvious intention to put the talents of the Von Braun team to the development of weapons for war.

Von Braun and his men, however, wanted only to continue their research on rockets, rockets to probe the upper atmosphere and venture into space and someday the planets. They had been diverted from this purpose once already, when Hitler became the leader of Germany and all such work went into the support of his ambitious wars.

Thus, Von Braun and more than a hundred members of his team were brought to the United States and were engaged in a rather leisurely paced research effort with some of the German V-2 rockets, launching them at the rate of about one or two a month at the Army's White Sands Missile Range. They were concerned only about research, while the government was comfortably engaged in peacetime endeavors and paying little attention to the prize it had captured in the German scientists.

The Soviets were all too aware of their failure to get Von Braun and his men, for they had pleaded, cajoled, and offered large amounts of money to them to go over to their side. But although they did not get the scientists themselves, they did seize a number of the German rockets from a captured production plant called the Mittelwerk in the Harz Mountains in Germany. In addition, they had a number of advanced rocket designs which the Americans had tried to get out of their secret cache in an underground cave. However, the territory where they were hidden was part of an area ceded to Russia at a summit meeting at Yalta. Although American soldiers retrieved most of the rocket plans before the deadline for Russian occupation, some were left behind.

So the Soviet Union secretly armed itself, plunging into the development of large rockets and studying the stolen nuclear documents. It took some bottles of rainwater to convey the news to the rest of the world. The Soviet Union also had the atomic bomb.

5

Sub in the Sagebrush

Out on a bleak, hot, almost desolated stretch of desert in Idaho a car slowly made its way down a dusty road, its occupants carefully surveying the area and making copious notes in a notebook. The men were from the Atomic Energy Commission and had made many such trips looking for just the right area for a special project.

If one had asked them what they wanted to build on their desert plot, the answer would have convinced the interrogator that they were affected by the desert sun. But it was true: they were looking for a place to build a submarine.

After looking at a number of areas, they settled on a stretch of desert larger than half the size of Rhode Island, covering 439,000 acres. The biggest concern of the AEC in choosing the site was safety; there were yet many unknowns about nuclear energy, and the agency wanted as much isolation as possible for the project in case of an accident.

The area was a former Naval ordnance testing ground located 20 miles east of Arco, Idaho, and it came to be referred to by that name. The other nearest towns were Idaho Falls and Blackfoot, some 45 miles away. It was far enough from these towns to provide a comfortable measure of safety from radiation leaks but close enough so that the employees of the station could make their homes there.

There was another consideration in the choice: with this much isolation from inhabited areas, sabotage would be difficult.

When the big trucks marked *Atomic Energy Commission* began to move into the area, they were greeted with considerable suspicion by the natives, most of the few of them there hunters and sheepherders and the like.

Their distrust was not lessened when they learned that "those scientists" had ordered truckload after truckload of disposable diapers. But later the AEC explained that the diapers were used to sop up radioactive liquids, having been found to be just perfect for this task.

The installation that went up in the Valley of the Lost Rivers was named the National Reactor Testing Station. Here, under Rickover's direction, a land-based prototype of the submarine reactor was to be built. This version would be called the Mark I; the actual sub reactor would be designated Mark II and would be a duplicate as the proper design was worked out.

Soon a few buildings, modern pyramids with 10-foot-thick concrete walls, began to rise from the desert floor. One of the buildings would house a materials-testing reactor, where materials which would go into the submarine reactor would be tested. Another was a chemical processing plant, in which unburned uranium was separated from radioactive waste. Yet another housed a number of research activities, including an experimental breeder reactor, from which the scientists hoped to create more fuel out of the atomic pile than was consumed in the process.

Yet another, a strange tall building more than 1,000 miles from any ocean, contained the actual working section of a submarine built far from any shipyard. It had been at Rickover's own insistence that the reactor be built inside a submarine hull; he wanted no arguments after it was built over whether it would fit inside a ship or not.

The vessel was, of course, not completely intact. It lacked the parts which would have taken it to sea, the crew quarters, the conning tower, the bow, stern, diving planes, and the like. But in the engine rooms the controls were real and the equipment was complete.

Not only were these portions realistic, but they actually rode their own sea. They were surrounded by water in a tank containing almost 200,000 gallons of water, to further the simulation.

The plan was to do the work of research and development concurrently. As the AEC's Argonne Laboratories in Chicago developed the basic principles on the reactor, Westinghouse and its subcontractors already were working on the equipment. These pieces were sent to Arco, fitted into the Mark I assembly, tested, and revised if necessary.

The construction of the Mark I was one of the most demanding tasks American enterprise had ever seen. Because of the radioactivity, the welds in the water circulation system had to be extremely reliable—in fact, leaking no more than one drop of water in a hundred years. While most welding jobs take seven or eight passes with a torch for extra strength, these took thirty-three passes, and as long as three days on each area. Some aspects took actual feats of heroism to complete, such as a difficult joint in which the welders went in without masks, knowing they would have injuries severe enough to require hospitalization because of it. The strange submarine was built in record time.

As the vehicle took shape and its purpose was explained to the neighboring townspeople, it receded in importance in the eyes of the local inhabitants and they once again went about their normal pursuits. The hunters returned, their fears of radioactive antelope dispelled.

The management at the Electric Boat Division of General Dynamics Corporation, chosen to build the submarine itself, had its difficulties at first also. The company marked off an area for its atom submarine work, which it nicknamed Siberia, and top-secret clearances were necessary to get in. But here also there was some initial fear of the project, as evidenced by the refusal by several insurance companies to insure the workers associated with it.

But the company itself was enthusiastic about the project. Fortuitously for the Navy, one of the foremost submarine designers in the country had gone to General Dynamics when he retired from the Navy. Rear Admiral Andrew I. McKee, with his staff of 140 men, is credited with much creative engineering in the solution of some of the new problems of the atomic submarine.

Although the primary program was the Mark I and II water-cooled reactor design, Rickover decided to hedge his bet by continuing work on another approach. This was the submarine intermediate reactor (SIR), which would operate with neutrons of considerably higher speeds than the Mark I and would use liquid sodium as a coolant instead of water. A contract was signed with General Electric for development of this reactor, which it would build at its Knolls Atomic Power Laboratory. Here also, a land-based prototype locked in a submerged submarine hull would be constructed, while General Dynamics built the submarine for which it was intended. However, it would be found years later that this approach was not as satisfactory as the Mark I, and the project would be discarded.

It was ironic that the actual method used to convert the energy from the reactor into power for a submarine was an age-old process long discarded in the propulsion of naval vessels. This was steam, which had been considered outmoded forty years before because of the dangers associated with its operation and the cumbersome equipment it required.

The main engines of the atomic submarine were to be essentially ordinary steam turbines, of the same kind of design that had been used on surface vessels in the past. The release of high-pressure steam on the blades of the turbine turned the ship's propellers.

Nuclear energy was, in fact, simply a better way of making steam. In the pressurized water reactor—the Mark I—ordinary water was used to slow down or moderate the neutrons. As it performed this function, it was heated to very high temperatures because of the friction caused by the neutrons. This hot, radioactive water is called the "primary coolant." Through a heat exchanger, the heat in this water was used to convert a secondary tank of water to steam. The steam would not be radioactive because it would never come into direct contact with the primary coolant. To ensure that the radioactivity did not escape, the primary coolant or pressurized water system was completely sealed. Even the pumps used to circulate the water were sealed in containers or "canned" like food on the grocery store shelf.

With design on the submarine and reactor progressing nicely, Rickover decided to make a presentation to the Joint Chiefs of Staff on his concept. These top military men were impressed, and in August, 1950, President Harry S. Truman gave the official go-ahead for an atomic submarine.

As he signed the historic bill, Truman announced publicly for the first time the tremendous revolution taking place in submarine technology: "The *Nautilus* will be able to move under the water at a speed of more than twenty knots. A few pounds of uranium will give her ample fuel to travel thousands of miles at top speed. She will be able to stay under water indefinitely. Her atomic engine will permit her to be completely free from the earth's atmosphere. She will not even require a breathing tube to the surface."

Nautilus was a fitting name for the first atomic submarine. "Nautilus" is also the name of a pearly, spiral-shelled mollusk. Oliver Wendell Holmes wrote: "This is the ship of pearl, which, poets feign, sails the unshadowed main."

The famed dreamer and fiction writer Jules Verne, whose fantasies about rockets and submarines have proven to be extremely prophetic, created a mythical submarine *Nautilus* in his popular *Twenty Thousand Leagues Under the Sea,* in 1869.

The name had a proud place in the annals of naval history as well as legend. *Nautilus* was the name given by Robert Fulton to his platter-shaped submarine around the turn of the nineteenth century. There were two American submarines named the *Nautilus,* one launched in 1913, another in 1930. This latter had a special place in the Navy record book; it was the first American ship to sink a Japanese aircraft carrier in World War II, the 10,000-ton *Sorya* at Midway. It also landed raiders before the invasions of Tarawa, Makin, and Attu, but collapsed and was scrapped because of old age in 1946. And prophetically, *Nautilus* was the name of the submarine a famous British naval figure, Sir Hubert Wilkins, used in his attempt to go under the polar ice cap in 1931.

This venture failed and would not be accomplished for many years.

The *Nautilus* had the official Naval designation of SS(N) 571, the (N) standing for nuclear. The *Nautilus* was more than 300 feet long, with the lead-shielded reactor in the center of the vessel. Forwardmost toward her blunt prow was a torpedo room with six torpedoes inside. Behind this was the forward crew quarters, officers' stateroom, a comfortable wardroom lounge. Below these were the crew's mess and galley, all much more spacious than those in conventional submarines. Toward the center of the vessel and next to the shielded reactor section were the periscope room, the control center, and the attack center—the brains of the ship.

Behind the reactor compartment was a conventional diesel-electric plant and snorkel, which could be used in the unlikely event of trouble with the reactor or during maintenance periods. Aft of this was the maneuvering center and last the crew berthing, where comfortable bunks build into private cubicles rose three or four tiers high.

The long submerged operations of the vessel required design of a special air-conditioning system which would purify the air for reuse since no fresh air would be brought in each day by the snorkel. A special chemical compound, lithium hydroxide, was used to remove carbon dioxide produced by the crew as it breathed. Yet another chemical, activated charcoal, was used to collect other contaminants and remove odors.

As his organization grew, Rickover did not deviate from the spartan regime he had followed in leaner days. While others might have sought to build empires, choosing impressive offices and appurtenances, Rickover sought only to avoid the fuss and get on with the job.

As his staff expanded into other rooms in the Tempo 3 building, he had carpets stripped from the floor to work in wartime austerity. He wanted no comforts to create complacency, a deadly enemy of the kind of crash effort he demanded from his men.

His own pace was phenomenal. He appeared at the dilapidated, so-called "temporary" building near the Washington Monument at eight each morning, his slight frame housing a human dynamo as he prepared to tackle, head-on, the day's business. The day would be paced by rapid, staccato telephone calls, interspersed with intense interviews as he went about the job of selecting men for his organization. Lunch was a dieter's repast of fruit and soup, seeming hardly adequate for the energies it had to support.

Often after a full day's work, he would go directly to the train station or airport for a trip to Groton, Connecticut, or Pittsburgh or Schenectady, where he would have conferences with contractors. After concluding his business, he would hop the next conveyance back to Washington, appearing the next morning for work seemingly completely refreshed and ready for the new day.

One of his specialties was cutting through red tape, and he took advantage of his two-hatted status to

71

save much time, writing and answering letters to himself while at the same time fulfilling all the requirements for interagency coordination.

His dealings with American industry are legend. It is said that he once awakened a corporation president at two o'clock in the morning to discuss an idea which had suddenly occurred to him. Another company executive he interrupted while in a minor operation. And it has been reported that he sent a Canadian mounted policeman after another who was vacationing at a Canadian lake.

But the kind of progress that he was after brooked no delay. When a metallurgical firm said it could not have a certain processing plant operating for at least a year, Rickover told them in no uncertain terms that he expected it on line in ten weeks. Needless to say, he was right. Another company manufacturing a certain component estimated a fourteen-month delivery time; after an abrasive Rickover treatment, it was ready in ten months.

He was not always complimentary about the performance of American industry, either. There were a number of weaknesses in equipment that was delivered for the project, and its manufacturers were rewarded with perhaps the stiffest tongue-lashing they had ever known. At one point in the program, it has been reported, he demanded a "permission to degrade specifications." In other words, if a contractor was not going to produce goods of the quality he had promised to do, he would have to give a good reason for it. Otherwise, the best performance was expected. Needless to say, few contractors had the courage to put a request form for permission to degrade specifications on the peppery admiral's desk.

Rickover summed up for the Washington *Star* his own feelings in this way: "For man to take full advantage of modern technology he must raise his standards of knowledge and performance. The high temperatures, pressures, and speeds needed today require the use of materials close to their ultimate limits, and the consequences of failure become ever greater.

"Therefore, the utmost care must be taken in design, manufacture, installation, and operation. No carelessness can be tolerated anywhere in the entire chain, or the result may prove disastrous.

"Every person involved must constantly bear in mind that he is personally responsible for the entire ultimate result. It should be a mandatory requirement that every administrator be made responsible for personally directing in detail one of his projects. This would immediately show him the human and matériel pitfalls involved. He would not be able to sit at a desk issuing orders without understanding their real meaning."

Rickover had another argument for industry if a contractor wanted him to ease up on his requirements. He would ask them, "If you knew that your own sons would have to serve on that submarine would you design it my way or your way?"

Rickover's stringent requirements were adopted.

One thing Rickover insisted upon. Whereas in the aviation business the government footed 90 percent or better of the bill to construct facilities for produc-

73

tion, every dollar of the cost of building manufacturing facilities for the submarine reactor program was borne by the contractors themselves.

There were difficulties in staffing his organization, Rickover found. He saw immediately that he was faced with two alternatives: "raiding" other nuclear program offices or training his own men. If he tried to lure experienced engineers or scientists from other projects, it could only damage the country's potential in the nuclear energy field in the long run.

He expressed this philosophy in a Congressional hearing: "Any man in charge of a project who feels responsible for it must realize that an inherent part of his duties is to train people from the very start of the project. Of course, if one is assigned a project and is furnished all of the money he needs and all of the trained people required, he might as well go fishing because there is then nothing left to do. There is nothing difficult about running a project if one is given everything he needs."

Rickover adopted the procedure of getting only young people for his staff, many of whom were the best graduates from universities in the country. As time wore on, he worked out an arrangement with the deans of various engineering and scientific schools, who would recommend their best graduates for the atomic submarine project. A four-man board would interview each applicant separately, recommending only about one out of every four.

"We can't afford to have people around here who have reputations, but who don't work. We would rather have people who work hard and don't have the reputations," Rickover would say.

Rickover realized that there would be few engineers and scientists available for hire who would have training or experience in the design of nuclear power plants. In addition, experience with reactor studies or with the design of research reactors or plutonium production reactors would be of only minor value to the designer of a nuclear power plant. From the outset, he realized he would have to train the people in his own organization and to arrange for the training of those in the contractors' organizations as well.

The first thing he did was to arrange a special twelve-month course in nuclear engineering at the Massachusetts Institute of Technology especially for Naval officers. The officers, also handpicked by Rickover and his staff, were either graduates of the Naval Academy or engineering majors of civilian universities, all of whom had received three years of postgraduate work in engineering.

Next, in late 1949, Rickover was instrumental in establishing the Oak Ridge School of Reactor Technology for the purpose of giving advanced nuclear training to members of his own organization, AEC contractors, governmental agencies, Navy yards and shipyards. The schools were designed to teach future reactor designers information which at the time existed only in the minds and notebooks of the Manhattan Project scientists and engineers.

Rickover laid out a program to train personnel in

all of the necessary basic fields and specialties, literally bringing them up from scratch. He arranged for special lecture courses and series at each laboratory and shipyard, and searched for universities nearby for applicable academic training. As personnel within the Naval reactors branch became trained in nuclear engineering, they gave several series of technical lectures to top management and engineering personnel of the first contractors in the Naval reactors program. At the Westinghouse-operated Bettis Laboratory, many people were employed for the sole purpose of training subcontractors in the highly specialized work being done. In the same manner, Electric Boat Division, being the first shipyard to become experienced in dealing with nuclear-powered vessels, was used to train personnel of other shipyards as they entered the field.

Thus, hundreds of scientists, design engineers, plant operators, medical officers, and maintenance personnel acquired, in a Rickover curriculum, an education in a field never before taught.

Rickover was permitted special leeway by the personnel offices of the Navy in choosing Naval officers. Out of the new ranks of engineering-duty-only officers each year, about fifteen would be invited to come in for an interview. Out of these, four or five would be asked to stay. Most of the young Reserve officers chosen by Rickover agreed to stay on for four years instead of the usual two or three, and then many stayed on as civilian employees of the branch.

The interviews conducted by the unpredictable

admiral are part of the Rickover legend. In some interviews, it has been reported, the prospective employee was seated on a chair whose front legs were shorter than the back ones. Then the squirming young engineer would face a barrage of questions.

The young man would be asked if he was resourceful, to which he almost always replied yes. Then he would be told to suppose he was on a sinking boat with five other men. How would he convince them he was the only one who should be saved?

Yet another story is that Rickover would ask the interviewee to name the last six books he had read. Upon receiving the names, he then would ask for the authors, which he would check. Commander William R. Anderson, who would one day be skipper of the *Nautilus* on its historic polar voyage, felt that he had flunked this part of the test cold. Caught completely unaware, Anderson, although he had a literary bent, could not think of the names of any of the books he had read during the past two years.

Anderson left the office dejectedly, feeling he had lost his chance to get into the nuclear submarine program. However, he proved his own resourcefulness by sending a complete list the next day, and ultimately he was accepted.

While such stories abound, it also is known that the admiral would subject the interviewees to long and searching interrogation on technical subjects. And his tactics were not as cruel as they may have sounded. By subjecting the men to such situations, he found those who could think quickly in a tough spot, overcome temporary setbacks, and retain their poise in an adverse situation. These qualities he felt important in the leaders of the new fleet.

Once aboard, he was an unorthodox administrator of his staff. In some cases sacred Navy protocol was laid aside as higher-ranking officers found themselves taking orders from more experienced but lower-grade Navy men. Top slots were often as not given to civilians, to avoid the two-year job reshuffle of career officers in the Navy. As Rickover said of the career men, "It takes an officer a year to understand his job. Then he works at it for six months and spends the next six months worrying about his next assignment."

He was tough on his staff, demanding and receiving excellence. One frustrated scientist was intercepted coming out of Rickover's office in a blind rage after an argument. The scientist had been arguing over something Rickover wanted done, laying out "incontrovertible proof" that the feat could not be accomplished.

"He just looked at me like I was a mental defective," the scientist roared. But this was part of Rickover's method of operation; he'd needle them into such a rage that they would go out and do the job just to spite him.

But in the magnitude of their accomplishments, the camaraderie among the men grew, and they developed a fierce pride in the team and its leader. For them, he fought for the highest Civil Service ratings and Navy promotions. And in rare moments he spoke in tones of highest praise and affection of them. "There is no one in my organization who couldn't get a bigger salary outside, but few leave," he said with pride.

Early in the battle for his program, Rickover kept an important lesson in mind. Perhaps thinking back to the way a Congressman from Chicago had changed his life, he kept a respectful eye on the United States Congress. Later, Representative James E. Van Zandt of Pennsylvania related a meeting he had with the then Captain Rickover.

"When I joined the Joint Committee immediately after my separation from the Navy back in 1946, I was told there was a fellow in the Navy Department by the name of Rickover who was very much interested in the development of a nuclear-powered submarine. Having been a sailor in the Navy when they had coal ships and knowing the problems we have when we take on fuel oil today, I asked about this nuclear power in ships and was given a complete rundown," Van Zandt said.

"It was a matter of a year or more until I met Admiral Rickover and said to him, 'What can I do?' He said, 'Just keep quiet and get reelected.'

"That was the beginning of a long period of friendship I have enjoyed with the admiral. He has made many friends and he has made many enemies, but he has had one objective and that is the development of nuclear power, not alone for the submarine, but for the other types of craft so necessary to the Navy," Van Zandt said.

Not long after the *Nautilus* project was barely under way, Rickover would need those friends.

6

A Fast Ride Somewhere

There was excitement around Tempo 3 in the early 1950's as the program progressed with no apparent difficulties in sight. The atmosphere attracted a number of good young scientists and engineers working on other projects. They were eager to drop their conventional engineering and research projects for the stimulus of a new, unusual challenge and to work with the wiry human dynamo who was obviously going somewhere.

In addition to the design of the submarine and the reactor, there were other important details to consider. Not only did *Nautilus* have to prove her seaworthiness; she had to prove that the atomic submarine could perform better than conventional submarines under attack.

All the parts and systems considered for the *Nautilus* were put through grueling tests. Some were

81

sent to Arco, where they were put in the materials-testing reactor to see if they could stand up to the extreme heat and radioactivity. Others were pulled, pushed, compressed, shaken, and vibrated to determine the limits of their strength.

Scale models of the *Nautilus* were constructed, complete with simulated machinery having many of the characteristics of the actual planned equipment. These were set at depth in the Chesapeake Bay and blasted with depth charges, then examined. A World War II submarine, the *Ulua,* was fitted out with *Nautilus* equipment and submerged, and it too became the target of depth charges. Remotely operated moving cameras recorded the shock and the effect on the systems inside. The information was fed back to Tempo 3, and new plans were drawn up where necessary.

The reactor design itself, those on the project admitted, was not perhaps the most advanced or best conceivable. However, the urgency which underlaid his planning brought Rickover to a decision: If they stopped and listened to all the technical experts and others who came to them with advice, they would never have a nuclear submarine. The design was frozen—that is to say, a point was reached in which no further changes would be made—and actual construction began.

Yet another test had to do with the capabilities of the men who would man the sub themselves. Up until that time, no group of men had been submerged, and thus cooped up, for such a long period of time as was envisioned for *Nautilus'* missions. Would the men become bored, restless? Would their constant contact with one other, with no outside diversion, make them irritable and result in arguments and perhaps actual fights? How would all this affect their performance?

The Navy undertook to answer these questions in a simulated *Nautilus* mission. A fleet submarine, docked at New London, was submerged with 22 volunteers on board for about six weeks. The test, called Operation Hideout, showed that the crew could function successfully over this period of time. In addition, the oxygen-purifying equipment planned for the *Nautilus* was proven workable, and plans were made for its installation into the nuclear submarine.

In the summer of 1951 the first rumble of real trouble was heard in Tempo 3. The problem was not technical, but in some ways even more serious.

The Navy, like other military services, follows a system of promotion in which senior officers meet on selection boards to pick from lists of qualified officers those who will be promoted to the next higher rank. All of the officers who remain on the list without promotion are said to have been "passed over." If a man is considered and passed over twice, he must retire from the service. Although no one could think of a better way of doing the job, the services admitted that the process could be arbitrary and personal according to who sat on the particular selection board.

Rickover, not in command of a capital ship and as an engineering duty officer not likely ever to be, differed greatly from the others whose names were in the category of "captains" available for promotion to rear admiral. His work in nuclear engineering was not understood by many of the senior officers of the Navy, many of whom had an outright prejudice against the work he was doing to change their way of doing things. In addition, his own personality, sharp-tongued, impatient where he saw incompetence, was not considered properly fitted for line command. In fact, those around him said with awe, "He sticks to the straight line, even if it bisects six admirals."

On July 2, 1951, a Navy selection board passed over Rickover for the first time. The action caused some stir among his admirers, and scientists and Congressmen, including the chairman of the Joint Committee on Atomic Energy, wrote protesting letters to Navy Secretary Dan Kimball. The joint committee had an especially authoritative voice, being composed of both Senators and Representatives and having in its membership some of the keenest minds in the Congress. They were assured that the action probably was an oversight, and that he would be promoted in the next meeting of the board the following year.

Rickover's supporters were uneasy, but they accepted this assurance. During the next months, all seemed relatively calm as the work progressed without any great setbacks. A heartening note was the fact that the Navy seemed to be becoming really convinced that nuclear power was indeed the hope of the future; in April, 1952, Rickover's group was told to go ahead with the design of a nuclear-powered aircraft carrier.

As with the submarine reactor, the group decided

to construct a land-based prototype of one of the huge aircraft carrier's propulsion units. As a secondary benefit, the prototype could be used to demonstrate the feasibility of using nuclear power to make electricity for civilian use, for lighting homes and streets.

Meanwhile, the keel-laying of the *Nautilus,* a traditional ceremony for every important ship, was scheduled for June 14, Flag Day, 1952. President Harry S. Truman led a long list of officials at the event. Almost unnoticed, sitting in a back row on the stand, was a slight man in a gray business suit. As always, Rickover shunned the limelight.

Truman announced to the world the importance of the *Nautilus,* saying: "This vessel is the forerunner of atomic-powered merchant ships and airplanes, of atomic power plants producing electricity for factories, farms, and homes.

"The day that the propellers of this new submarine first bite into the water and drive her forward will be the most momentous day in the field of atomic science since that first flash of light down in the desert seven years ago," he continued.

"The military significance of this vessel is tremendous. The engine of the *Nautilus* will have as revolutionary an effect on the navies of the world as did the first oceangoing steamship one hundred and twenty years ago. But the peaceful significance of the *Nautilus* is even more breathtaking. When this ship has been built and operated, controllable atomic power will have been demonstrated on a substantial scale," the President said.

For the first time, Truman gave some idea of the capability of the vessel, still highly classified. However, he told the audience that its speed underwater would be greater than 20 knots and that only a few pounds of uranium would be needed to sustain her for thousands of miles at top speed. She would be able to stay underwater indefinitely, completely free of the earth's atmosphere, with not even a breathing tube to the surface.

Then the chairman of the Atomic Energy Commission, Gordon Dean, gave special praise to Rickover, saying, "There are many persons who have played a role in the events which have led to this ceremony, but if one were to be singled out for special notice, such an honor should go to Captain H. G. Rickover, whose talents we share with the Bureau of Ships, and whose energy, drive, and technical competence have played such a large part in making this project possible."

About a month later, back in Washington, Rickover received an urgent telephone message summoning him to the office of the Secretary of the Navy at the Pentagon, across the river in Virginia. Dressed in his customary civilian gray, he bustled through the ranks of uniformed officers in the corridors of the huge, five-sided building to the Secretary's office.

As he entered, he found the room crowded with people, who turned expectantly as he entered. With questioning eyes he turned to Navy Secretary Dan Kimball, who was advancing toward him with a beaming face. "The Navy's giving you another medal, Rick," he said.

As the room quieted, Kimball conferred a gold star on the bewildered captain, in lieu of a second Legion of Merit. In reading the citation, the Navy Secretary noted that "displaying exceptional talents in the field of mobile power reactors and exercising unceasing drive and energy, Captain Rickover, more than any other individual, is responsible for the rapid development of the nuclear ship program."

The citation also spoke of how Rickover had held tenaciously to his goal through discouraging frustration and opposition, and had in spite of these been able to see that the laying of the keel of the world's first nuclear-powered ship was done well in advance of its original schedule. It spoke also of his managerial ability, saying "his careful and accurate planning, his technical knowledge and ability to clarify and resolve problems arising between the Atomic Energy Commission, the Bureau of Ships and civilian contractors have proven a contribution of inestimable value to the country's security and reflect great credit upon Captain Rickover and the Naval service."

It truly appeared that Rickover's star was in the ascendancy. The award was the first time the Navy had conferred the Legion of Merit on an engineering duty officer since the war and was in itself a great honor. Rickover had received public recognition for his work, and the Pentagon press corps began to write stories about the intriguing nuclear reactor project and the men who worked on it.

But the very next day after the gold medal ceremony, the Navy selection board met again. In a secret session, the nine admirals on the board elevated thirty captains to the rank of rear admiral. Rickover was not one of them.

The outraged uproar which followed the meeting of the board started on Capitol Hill in the offices of the Joint Committee on Atomic Energy, spread to the Atomic Energy Commission, and ended in angry tirades in the ear of the Navy Secretary. Newspaper articles criticized the Navy in strong language. A national newsmagazine bluntly called it "brazen prejudice," and went on to praise Rickover.

The action meant that Rickover would have to retire at the age of fifty-two, in his own prime and before his project was completed. The excuses presented by the Navy were not convincing. Some muttered that the captain's talents were "too specialized" for the high rank. Others admitted that personalities probably played a great part in the decision; one junior Naval officer revealed that he had actually been warned not to work for Rickover, that he'd jeopardize his career with the association.

A few supporters started a full-scale crusade, among them a junior Senator from Washington, who as a member of the House of Representatives had been on the Joint Congressional Committee on Atomic Energy. Senator Henry "Scoop" Jackson was a strong admirer of Rickover's and gladly went to bat for him, writing letters to the Navy top brass.

The Navy tried to smooth over the incident. A letter was dispatched to Senator Jackson, explaining that there are many fewer vacancies than there are qualified career men to fill them. Rickover, being an engineering duty officer, was in even greater competition because of the scarcity of admiral slots for that category, the Navy said. Yet, his admirers countered, wasn't he the most important man in what the President himself termed one of the most important developments in naval history?

The Navy also attempted to hold out a consolation prize. Rickover probably would be requested to continue with the Naval reactor project in some capacity as a civilian after his retirement, it said in a rather condescending manner. But everyone knew that he would not be nearly as effective in the intolerable position of working for someone else on his own project.

The morale in his group was extremely low. The action seemed to spell doom for the project; it seemed to be evidence that the opponents of nuclear power had won. The men who had come from industry, from universities, and from other posts in the service to dedicate their abilities to this man, with all the sacrifice of spare time and pleasure that it entailed, were shaken.

The knowledge throughout official Washington that Rickover had been passed over intruded another problem: Would a passed-over captain not apparently wanted by the Navy be able to get the same attention and response as did the up-and-coming director of the hottest project around?

Almost everyone who had dealt with Rickover at one time or another joined the foray, in one or the other camp. Those who had been insulted by his brusque manner or had seen his work a potential threat to the traditional way of doing things pooh-

poohed the whole thing. The selection process was the best possible, they said, and after all, everyone could not be promoted.

Others in this group whispered that Rickover really had not done so much—he was simply a figurehead for a group of experts who did all the work. Rickover himself would have been the first to admit that much credit should go to his men. But what his detractors failed to mention was that the assemblage of this team was due to his own perception and selectivity, and that his heading of the project was the reason for many of its members being on it. As one promising young engineer, who took a salary loss to work with Rickover, said, "I'm not sure where we're going to end up, but it's a fast ride somewhere."

There were rumors about his previous service record. Some of the top-line officers implied that his commands were not quite up to scratch; they joked about the rusty old submarine he had commanded, as if it were a thing of shame.

His chief support seemed to be in Congress. In the House the Representative from Chicago, Congressman Sidney Yates, voiced his feelings in a speech to his colleagues. He told them about the Gold Medal and the citation which said that Captain Hyman G. Rickover had accomplished "the most important piece of development work in the Navy." Then he told them that Rickover would have to retire the next June 30.

"At this time when we need every expert we have in the field of nuclear weapons, when we need knowledge, vision, and imagination, to compel this man to retire from active service is appalling. It is true that no one is indispensible, but in this instance Captain Rickover has exhibited, more than any other person in the Navy, the vision to adapt nuclear power to naval purposes," Yates said.

As is often true in either house of Congress, the chamber was not crowded. But Yates knew that every word he spoke would be recorded in the *Congressional Record* and read by every office on Capitol Hill the next morning.

"To my mind he deserves the promotion which would permit him to remain in the Navy. Even more important, however, it seems to me that it is in the best interests of the nation that he be given the promotion in order that his talents may continue to be used for national defense."

Yates' speech was attracting attention from the galleries, and the press gallery above the speaker's rostrum began to fill as the word got out that an interesting speech was being made.

"Mr. Speaker, only God and the members of the Naval selection board know what occurred during the deliberations of the board. It is well known that members of the fighting forces of the Navy are given preference in promotion over members of equal rank in other branches of the Navy service. Disregarding that fact, however, in this case rank discrimination must have been present, for six officers in the engineering branch junior to Captain Rickover received promotions to rear admiral. It seems to me, Mr. Speaker, that the Armed Services Committee of the Senate should certainly inquire as to why Captain

Rickover was passed over again, before it confirms appointments made by the President on recommendation of the Naval selection board," Yates suggested to a now intensely interested audience.

The procedure in which the Senate considered the President's nominations for promotion of members of the armed services was almost automatic. The lists drawn up by the selection boards of the services went directly to the White House, where they were signed by the President and sent on to the Senate Armed Services Committee. In almost rubber-stamp fashion, the committee would approve the list and send it to the Senate floor, where once again it would get swift and automatic approval. The suggestion that the committee hold up the entire list of promotions over this one case was radical indeed.

Other Congressmen took up the fight. Congressman John McCormack, who would later become Speaker of the House of Representatives, pointed out that Navy selection boards could have their human weaknesses and prejudices. "Can't they make errors of judgment and give their friends a little break?" he asked. "And if they can give a break to someone who is a friend of theirs, can they not give somebody else a bad break sometimes?"

Representative Melvin Price, a member of the Joint Committee on Atomic Energy, gave his forthright opinion: "If the policy of selection reacts in such a manner that it does harm to a man of the capacity and talents of Captain Rickover, it must in my opinion be a bad policy and something should be done about it."

The newsmen took up the fight in earnest. "The Navy's upper brass has never looked worse," one wrote. The Navy was accused of prejudice against specialists, of lagging far behind the Army and the Air Force in its recognition of the tremendous achievements of its engineers, scientists, and other experts in fields other than warfare. If it treated Rickover this way, it could never again attract men of high scientific and technical caliber, they warned.

This point had teeth in it. Already there were rumblings within the Naval reactors division of inpending resignations. And big industry was all too ready to offer these bright scientific minds high salaries to join their companies.

Finally, the Senate Armed Services Committee, one of the most powerful committees, if not the most powerful single committee, in Congress, called a special hearing on the Rickover case. The Navy presented a long statement on the history of the Navy nuclear program, giving credit for the accomplishments of the program to almost everyone but Rickover, even some of those who had attempted to hinder it most! The names of Rickover's superiors were mentioned frequently but without the background information on how Rickover had prepared a letter for signature by the Secretary of the Navy to get the program going, how he had pushed and pleaded to get these superiors to act. The statement also said that the nuclear-power billet in the Bureau of Ships was a captain's billet, and that the Navy had a number of well-qualified engineering duty captains ready to take over, some of whom had been in the program since its inception. Who these might have been remained a mystery to the Naval reactors group. They also scoffed at the idea that the Navy really believed that the post of director of what the Navy itself had just recently called "the most important piece of development work in the Navy," was suited only to a captain.

Throughout the uproar, Rickover himself had remained relatively silent, perhaps deeply hurt but refusing to take advantage of the publicity which was offered him. Characteristically he refused interviews and photographers, except in the discussion of the program itself. When Congressmen called him and asked him to come for private talks about his case, he refused, saying he did not feel it was proper for him to have such conversations.

Some of the other members of the Naval reactors group were less reluctant, however. At the request of several Senators, they traveled to Capitol Hill to relate the full story behind the Navy's statements.

Senator Henry Jackson, armed with the details, himself became a witness before the Senate Armed Services Committee. He told the august body that he was not necessarily an advocate of Captain Rickover, having only met him through his work on the Joint Committee on Atomic Energy. But he stressed that he was an advocate of any program which would produce scientific victories for the United States.

In a very convincing speech, Jackson described how scientific progress had spelled military strength before, with the development of radar early in World War II and finally with the development of the atomic bomb. "But there is one lesson you learn almost as soon as you look into the problem of research and development for the sake of national security; scientific genius is not to be found and developed solely through the ordinary course of military conformity and the philosophy of never sticking your neck out. If slavish acceptance of barnacle-encrusted views, if going along with past and traditional methods, if striving to make one's manners and methods go along in complete uniformity with the rest of the service—if these things are to be the price of promotion in the technical branches of the services, I honestly fear for the security of our country," Jackson told them.

He described how Hitler had failed in harnessing scientific minds; how in requiring conformity he had driven out some of the best scientists of the century. "Toeing the line, total obedience, and total conformity may be essential to success in battle—but they are not the factors which make for great forward strides in technical battles," he said.

The thoughts could have been Rickover's own. Often he had remarked that the kind of blind obedience taught by the military in its acadamies such as the Naval Academy at Annapolis was useless in the scientific laboratory and on the engineering drawing board. He also had said privately to a friend, "Any military man who uses his head is going to get his block knocked off."

Jackson argued home his point: "Original minds, men with imagination, men with the driving genius to get revolutionary things done, must be able to find a place in the armed services—and they must be able to bring forward and advocate their fresh ideas without fear of reprisal. Today, I believe the case of Captain Rickover is a prime example of how not to treat splendid creative technical officers in the armed services."

He pointed out that the Air Force, which had a similarly important project, had a general in charge of its work, and the project was not going nearly as well as Rickover's. "The whole project has been treated as an orphan," he declared.

More and more voices were raised, including many of the top officials of the industrial firms with whom Rickover had dealt. He'd been sharp with them at times, and critical too, but they respected him and knew that in the long run his way had been best.

The White House became increasingly concerned about the case and called for action by the Secretary of the Navy to resolve the situation. Secretary Robert B. Anderson, like his predecessor, Dan Kimball, also respected the captain and the work which he had accomplished. He studied the whole matter and searched for a means to avoid Rickover's retirement without completely counteracting the Navy's traditional selection system.

It was decided to convene a special selection board, which would be empowered to recommend that engineering duty captains could be retained for active duty for a period of one year. A requirement would be that one of these captains be experienced and qualified in the field of atomic-propulsive machinery for ships.

Another requirement would be that such captains would be eligible for consideration by a selection board the next July for promotion to rear admiral. That board also would be required to select for promotion to rear admiral "one engineering duty captain experienced and qualified in the field of atomic-propulsive machinery for ships." There was no question in anyone's mind who this one captain would be.

The solution seemed the best possible compromise, and the Senate passed the selection board's recommendations which it had held up. However, its members made it clear that they felt they had a binding promise from the Navy that it would promote the captain the next time around.

With relief, the men at the Naval reactor group returned to their work, which had suffered somewhat during the long, involved hassle. The bulk of the work was still ahead.

7

For Civilians Only

But it wasn't long before the rug was pulled out from another one of his projects, Rickover found. This time, it was the Joint Chiefs of Staff of the military services, perhaps spurred by considerations of economy and unable to see the need for nuclear power, who were responsible for the cancellation of the project. This was the large ship reactor or CVR, which originally had been approved by the Joint Chiefs. Convinced of the need for work on reactors of this size, Rickover and engineers at the Atomic Energy Commission had drawn up careful plans for a shore-based prototype of a single-shaft system, suitable for a large naval vessel such as an aircraft carrier. It was to be a breeder reactor, generating power and producing plutonium as atomic fuel at the same time.

On April 22, 1953, however, the word came from the White House. The National Security Council and the newly inaugurated President Dwight D. Eisenhower had decided to cancel the large ship reactor project from the defense program. In arriving at this decision, they were influenced by members of the Defense Department near the top level.

The decision was a blow to those who had worked long and hard on the project and to Rickover, who fully believed that the day would come when the large reactor would be urgently needed for the bigger Navy surface vessels. In addition, there was another major consideration. The reactor design was of such a size and type that it would be suitable for use as the basis for a civilian power plant. Although Rickover argued for this aspect also, the Defense Department turned a deaf ear.

According to the Defense Department, private industry should take on this project if it wanted it that much. Let one of the big electric companies foot the bill for the reactor, since it would be the one selling the electricity, its officials said.

Rickover was distressed. He knew that no single industrial company was ready to jump in and undertake such a project. The technology was too new, too complex, and too overwhelming for these civilian companies, who had no experience with nuclear energy matters. The high degree of classification during the early years of the development of atomic energy left the expertise concentrated in a small community of scientists and engineers, most of whom were in the AEC or military.

He appealed to his superiors at the Defense Department to hold up the decision to terminate the CVR project for a month or six weeks, so he could sound out some of the private companies on their interest in continuing the development of the large reactor on their own. The request was denied.

The Atomic Energy Commission took a different viewpoint, however. They were most concerned that the lead developed by the United States in the nuclear area would be lost if the work did not go on. What would be the image of the United States if it dropped its only project that would bring the benefits of atomic energy to all the people and continued only in its effort to manufacture weapons of great destruction? Many of the scientists were embittered. Mostly peaceful men, they had put their talents behind the wartime Manhattan Project with an eye to the future, when nuclear energy could be turned to the task of making life more productive for all people. Now, it seemed, there was no such intention by the leaders of the United States government.

At the urging of its top people, including AEC Commissioner Thomas E. Murray, a letter was sent to President Eisenhower by the acting chairman of the AEC, H. D. Smyth. He pointed out that the President himself had said, "The early development of nuclear power by the United States is prerequisite to our maintaining our lead in the atomic field."

Smyth urged him to allow the continuation of segments of the large ship and aircraft programs, even if they were not required for national security. "They are essential to the development of civilian power," he said. He also stressed the confidence the Atomic Energy Commission had in Rickover's approach. "We

101

are convinced that the pressurized light-water reactor, which is the heart of the planned large-ship propulsion unit, offers a promising avenue of approach which must be pursued vigorously if the nation is to get on with the job of attaining civilian power."

He pointed out the obstacles which lay in the way of private-financing work in the nuclear field. It was too early to expect private industry to assume a major part of the expensive, long-term development work that would have to be done.

The record, after all, was discouraging. The first atomic power project—the Monsanto Daniels Pile—began under the Manhattan Engineering District in 1946 at Oak Ridge. It failed a year later. A second atomic power project ran its course from 1948 through early 1950 at the General Electric Knolls Laboratory at Schenectady, New York. Once again, it was canceled. The reason this time was that the directors of the project could see ahead to the staggering costs looming over the horizon.

Then, in 1951, four groups of private companies had met together to study the prospects for privately financed projects. The meetings brought out a lot of enthusiasm but little money. However, the AEC felt that with government management and backing, these companies might be enticed into putting some funds into the project.

The President, a military man whose prime thought now was to bring the benefits of peace to the country, made his decision. On May 6, 1953, he wrote to the Atomic Energy Commission. The earlier action eliminating the large reactor project as a military requirement stands, he said. "However, I will adopt the recommendation that the pressurized light-water reactor and related research be continued, pending the availability of private financing in the interest of nuclear power development," he informed them.

All looked smooth now for the project. Rickover set right to work, drawing up a plan of action for the program, which was to develop a slightly enriched, light-water-cooled and moderated reactor concept, the same as that which had been planned for the naval aircraft carrier.

To everyone's amazement, however, it was now the Bureau of the Budget, ever mindful of the national pocketbook, which clamped down. It refused to grant the money needed to begin construction for facilities for the prototype plant. It looked as if they had won the war, only to be defeated at the last skirmish.

Once again, the story made its way to Congress, producing a strong reaction in the members of the Joint Committee on Atomic Energy. These men, who had dug so deeply into the nuclear development field to try to understand it, and who understood its ramifications in the world's political arena, took immediate action.

"It is possible that the relations of the United States with every other country in the world would be seriously damaged if Russia were to build an atomic power plant for peacetime use ahead of us," the chairman warned.

"The possibility that Russia might demonstrate her 'peaceful intentions' in the field of atomic energy while we are still concentrating on atomic weapons could be a major blow to our position in the world," he said. He also pointed out that the decision not to go ahead could even disrupt the continued operations of U.S. weapons plants. Friendly countries might cut off the vital uranium they now produced and sold to America.

Once again, Congress acted. It added $7,000,000 to the AEC budget for the construction of at least one atomic power plant designed to produce commercial electric power. However, it made it very clear that since it was, in effect, a Congressional project because it was not in the budget, it wanted to keep very careful tabs on it.

The Rickover plan was submitted. The reactor was to be sized to generate at least 60,000 kilowatts of useful electric energy. The program was first and foremost to be a civilian one, and no naval engineering was to be introduced if it would cause any delay in the program or increase the cost or affect the economical functioning of the reactor for its primary purpose as a central station power plant. Yet Rickover, and a few others, knew that the technology would be furthered. Ultimately, it might be needed.

While the Atomic Energy Commission decided to make no immediate public announcement, the news finally was disclosed in a speech that summer by Commissioner Murray. Addressing a meeting of Chicago electric companies, he said:

"I am very glad to be able to tell you officially today that the commission has embarked on a program to construct a full-scale power reactor. This is

America's answer—its significant peacetime answer—to recent Soviet atomic weapons tests. It should show the world that even in this gravest phase of arming for defense America's eyes are still on a peaceful future."

Murray's announcement brought a standing ovation from the audience, who more than anyone else saw the potential for the future. The news was received warmly in the newspapers and by the public, for it proved that at last, eight years after the dropping of the atomic bombs at Hiroshima and Nagasaki, the United States was taking concrete steps to turn this awful development to peace.

Supervision of the project was given to the AEC's Reactor Development Division, which immediately assigned it to the logical person, the one who knew most about it, Rickover.

While there was some grumbling about what the psychological effect might be of having a Navy man in charge of the project, Murray took a strong stand on this.

"Let me tell you that this choice was based solely on the admiral's unique experience and accomplishments in building propulsion reactors for the commission and for the Navy." And to others, he said, "The only Navy aspect which the admiral will bring to this work is his title."

Rickover turned to the job of selecting the proper industrial contractor to work with. This was extremely important, because the success or failure of their working relationship could have a profound effect on the future acceptance of atomic energy plants.

Hopping from one airplane to another, he began touring the East Coast in search of the right one. He visited contractors in Pennsylvania, South Carolina, Louisiana, New York, and New England, asking questions, casting an experienced and probing eye over their operations.

In March, 1954, the Duquesne Light Company of Pennsylvania was informed that its proposal had been accepted. The location of the plant would be on land that the company owned at Shippingport, about 25 miles from Pittsburgh. One day, it would provide the city of Pittsburgh with electrical power.

Ground was broken at Shippingport on Labor Day, 1954. The height of the nuclear core pressure vessel was 33 feet, and the reactor itself was 6 feet in diameter and 6 feet high.

In designing the plant, Rickover realized that it would be useless to proceed on such a venture unless it would result in a conservation of natural resources. If the production of electricity were too expensive, he realized, it would be unfeasible. In addition, the main purpose of the development of nuclear power was to halt the consumption of such things as coal and oil, which were being expended at a fantastic rate compared with the millions of years it took nature to produce them.

The admiral expressed his concern: "All modern industrial societies depend upon energy resources. The present rate of increase in the use of these resources, is about 10 percent per year in the United States.

"About one hundred years ago only 5 percent of

the energy we used came from gas, oil or coal; 1 percent came from water power, the rest came from the muscle power of human beings and animals. But today the story is quite different. Today only about 4 percent of the energy we use comes from human beings and animals, 1 percent from water power, and almost 95 percent comes from coal, oil, or gas."

What was the significance of this? He went on, "It is evident we are increasingly dependent upon artificial sources of energy. Again, in the last fifty years, the world has used more coal, oil, and gas than has been used previously in all history. If our rate of using fossil fuel sources continues at the rate we are using them now, in about one hundred years we can look to serious shortages. Therefore it is highly important that we develop alternative sources of energy.

"Atomic power gives us this means; that is why it is important. If we do not develop it now, if we do not take the time we have to get it so it can be useful, we will surely be caught short on energy resources," he declared.

Many people had the false impression that the advent of atomic power would mean an immediate decrease in their electric bills. Rickover hastened to explain that this was by no means the case, at least for the present. "Then why are we doing it?" they would ask.

"Because if you don't proceed with its development, you will never get comparable atomic power. I think you are being subjected to a distorted viewpoint when you hear all of these arguments for economic atomic power which have been figured so carefully that they predict the cost to a hundredth of a mill. The objective in developing atomic power is to develop an alternative source of energy for our fossil fuel resources which must eventually run out.

"From a purely logical standpoint," he pointed out, "we should never use coal or oil because they were created by solar energy 500,000,000 years ago. The oil we use each year took nature 14,000,000 years to create. You need only be a grammar school graduate and start doing a little computing to learn that no matter how much more oil we may find, we must eventually run out because the rate of creation of new fossil fuels is so slight. So no matter how large the bank account is, it can't keep up with the rate at which we are spending. On this basis, we should restrict the use of coal and oil for energy purposes, because it is very wasteful of our natural resources."

It was for this reason that Rickover was in favor of the new concept of "seed and blanket" for the Shippingport reactor. For if he had used enriched uranium as in the submarine reactors, he would still have been using substantial amounts of coal indirectly, because the process of enriching the fuel required a considerable quantity of electrical power. Obviously, if atomic power was to replace coal, there would be little point in using coal to make enriched uranium, then using this uranium to generate atomic power, he reasoned.

Thus, the plant was designed to produce as much energy as possible from natural uranium. The design chosen was referred to as the "seed blanket concept."

108

It uses a minimum of enriched U-235, actually about 75 kilograms, and a blanket of 14 tons of natural uranium. The idea is to keep the natural uranium in place as long as possible and to get all of the energy possible out of it. The energy comes from the one U-235 atom present in every 140 atoms of natural uranium, from the fast fissioning of U-238, and from the plutonium which is formed in the natural uranium in the reactor.

The fuel element used in the Shippingport reactor, which was named the PWR, for pressurized water reactor, was uranium oxide, a brownish powder. This powder is really uranium which has become completely rusted or oxidized. Once a metal is in the form of an oxide, it can't chemically absorb any more water.

This meant a great deal in terms of safety from water damage to the reactor. If for any reason the zirconium tubes which contain the uranium oxide pellets were to crack and expose the oxide to the water passing through the reactor, not much would happen. The powder would have no affinity for the water and could not absorb it.

The uranium powder is compressed into small pellets, and a number of them are put into zirconium tubes. Zirconium is a good structural material for nuclear reactor cores because it does not absorb neutrons.

The reactor itself actually was a huge collection of these tubes, which were assembled in groups of about 100 and stacked in the reactor one on top of another. Water was circulated at high pressure through the spaces between the tubes, then went to the heat exchanger and imparted its heat to the water there. This water was turned into steam, which in turn drove a turbine which drove a generator which made electricity.

As construction began on the Shippingport reactor and the work progressed, Rickover ran his organization with the same kind of tight control and urgency as if it were a top-priority military project. Indeed, there seemed no compromising with the standards he set for every job he undertook, whether it be the mothballing of old ships, the design of a top-secret nuclear attack submarine, or the construction of a nuclear plant to light a city.

The reactor project manager, Westinghouse Electric Company, soon found out that Rickover expected weekly reports on critical items and could be very testy if all his questions were not answered by them. Frequent meetings were called between Westinghouse, Duquesne, and Rickover, and his staff as work progressed and moved toward the point where the reactor would begin to produce power. Later, for almost ten months before full criticality was reached, Rickover demanded daily teletype messages to keep him up to date on important items such as welding, installation of components, labor problems, and other items which might affect the completion of the plant. This was not enough for him, however, and the days were marked by whirlwind visits from the energetic admiral.

The inevitable questions came from anxious citizens about the danger of radioactivity from the plant. "We don't want radioactivity in our water," some said. "What about the air around the plant?" asked others querulously.

Rickover was careful to explain the precautions he had insisted upon.

"The radiation problem comes from two factors," he explained. "These are neutrons and gamma rays. The neutrons are stopped when the reactor stops. You only have to worry about the neutron radiation while the reactor is running.

"The mass of a hydrogen atom is about the same as that of a neutron. Therefore, if you have about three feet of water in a tank outside the reactor pressure vessel, and that is what we do, you have protection. The water, of course, consists of hydrogen and oxygen. The hydrogen atoms in this tank slow down and finally stop the neutrons. I think that the shielding is so good that only one out of about every thirty billion neutrons gets outside that water tank," he declared.

"But what about the gamma rays, are they stopped by the water?" he would be asked.

"The reason I have split the shielding problem into two parts is because we actually solve the problem in two distinct parts. We took care of the neutrons by placing three feet of water around the reactor pressure vessel. That stops the neutrons. But for gamma rays, we need mass."

He continued: "For instance, about a half a mile of air roughly has enough mass to stop gamma rays. But a few inches of lead will also stop them. So will five feet or so of concrete. It is entirely a case of mass, and we have not been able to learn any simple way of stopping gamma rays other than by mass."

"But you don't put five feet of concrete on your ships, do you?" he would be asked.

The answer, obviously, was no. In the submarine reactor plant, where space was very tight, lead was used. "But for a shore plant such as Shippingport, we could just pile sufficient earth, say from ten to fifteen feet. However, the five feet of concrete is the most practical."

The admiral also would explain an unusual fact about shielding and radiation. Shielding follows what is known in mathematics as an exponential law. If something can be shielded with five feet of concrete, it only takes one-tenth this thickness to make the shielding twice as effective. While this makes it easy to shield for bigger power plants, it also means that even if the power plant is small, a large amount of shielding is needed. Thus, with the present state of knowledge, it would be almost impossible to design an atomic power plant for an automobile.

The Shippingport reactor would one day meet and surpass all the hopes that the AEC and Congress had for it, becoming the basis for the technology of almost all succeeding atomic reactors. Its design was to be copied in the United States and abroad. The pioneering step of using uranium oxide would be followed by others. The seed and blanket concept, in which the control rods were installed in the seed only but adequately controlled the whole nuclear pile, was outstandingly demonstrated. It contributed much to the fields of nuclear physics, heat transfer, metallurgy, hydraulics, reactor control and equipment.

While grappling with the design problems of the moment, Rickover's eye always was to the future.

Several hundred instruments were installed inside the core of the Shippingport reactor, so that the engineers outside, safe from the heat and radiation inside, could know exactly what was happening in the core. Without this core and plant instrumentation, Rickover later said, "there would be no point in building a reactor, since I would not be developing or proving out advanced technology—technology which will benefit the entire reactor art." It was, perhaps, the ability to take the broader view which made him so successful in the details of the smaller steps.

At the same time that Rickover was fighting for the life of the large reactor project, there was exciting news from Arco, where the land-based prototype for the nuclear submarine was becoming a reality. On May 31, 1953, the first powered operation began. On June 23, 1953, it was brought to full power.

The test, which began at 8:15 that evening, was to run for 24 hours. During this time, engineers would gather important first information on the sustained operation of the nuclear reactor and obtain data on reactor physics and the reliability of the nuclear plant.

When the test was about to begin, Rickover was in Pittsburgh, conferring on the Shippingport project with some interested light companies. He immediately jumped on a plane and made his way to the AEC National Reactor Testing Station in the desert.

In spite of the high degree of excitement among the project officials, the test began smoothly. Time passed, and like the submarine it would one day power, the nuclear reactor caused not a ripple.

All went so well, in fact, that Rickover was struck

by an idea as he stood watching the skeletal submarine form, bound to the land in spite of the
tremendous energies being generated inside. Beckon-
ing to one of the staff, he uttered a strange request.
Did they have any charts of the North Atlantic
handy?

Knowing from experience that it was foolhardy if
not suicide to one's ego to question a Rickover
request, the staff rounded up complete nautical
charts of the North Atlantic and spread them around
the control room of the Mark I reactor as he directed.
The track for a submerged ocean crossing was drawn.
As the observers watched awestruck, Rickover
plotted a great circle course from Nova Scotia to
Ireland.

As the successive watches reported on duty, they
began to compete in the game to simulate a great
ocean crossing. Figuratively, the Mark I was kept
plunging ahead in the ocean depths, never surfacing,
never shutting down her power plant. Once or twice
she had to cut back to two-thirds or half-power as
engineering adjustments were made, but the spirit of
racing across the ocean to a new record was high, and
in each case, the "crew" moved quickly. They did not
want to be responsible for delaying the crossing any
more than necessary.

A triumphant message was sent to the top brass in
Washington as "landfall" was made on Ireland.
Puzzled, perhaps, the Pentagon duly congratulated
the desert submariners on their historical voyage.
Although the Defense Department left the duration
of the voyage classified since it might reveal secret

information about the speed of the nuclear submarines, they made it clear that all records had been smashed. It demonstrated emphatically the inherent reliability and safety of the system, in a manner which brought home the message much more strongly to the Navy men who needed more convincing than they would have received from a mere one-day test.

Six months later, the *Nautilus* submarine was officially launched at Groton, Connecticut. The idea of a nuclear submarine was beginning to attract a great deal of interest in Washington, and a nine-car special train left the Capitol for Groton, loaded with dignitaries who wanted to associate themselves with the project. Some 12,000 spectators crowded the docks.

The day, January 22, was rather dismal, fog hanging over everything and obscuring the view of those distant from the boat. *Nautilus*' first skipper, Commander Eugene Parks Wilkinson, stood on the bow. A speakers' platform was decorated with bunting and crowded with Navy and political figures who praised the project during the ceremonies. In the front row was Rickover, wearing a uniform for the first time in months but taking no part in the ceremony, sitting stiffly as he heard praise for his work.

"The *Nautilus* is a symbol of man's dreaming. His bright dreams, certainly, and if man is not wise, his nightmares, too," Admiral Robert Carney, the Chief of Naval Operations said.

He noted that *Nautilus* was but the first of a radical new type of naval vessel. Before it would gain acceptance, however, it would be tested in the grueling processes of the fleet's operational evaluation, in the time-honored tradition of the Navy. Only then would the true future of the nuclear submarine be determined.

At 10:57, January 21, 1954, Mrs. Dwight D. Eisenhower took a swing at the *Nautilus* with a champagne bottle. At the advice of an admiral, "Hit it good and hard, Mrs. Eisenhower," she did, and the *Nautilus* slipped into the water.

8

Under Way on Nuclear Power

The date set for the first builder's trial of the *Nautilus* was January 17, 1955, only a few weeks later than the original date promised by its program manager. The long gray vessel lay alongside Pier Charlie at the General Dynamics' Electric Boat Division dock in the Thames River as the passengers filed aboard. The ship would be extremely crowded for her first trip, taking on about sixty civilian technical experts who would check every piece of equipment as it operated. In addition, it had its full crew of more than a hundred. The captain was Commander Eugene Wilkinson, who had had extensive special training for his post. Next to him on the bridge was a slight, graying figure in a gray suit and no hat, his hair rumpled by the crisp January breeze.

After all were on board, the order went out to take in the line. Commander Wilkinson ordered, "Rudder amidship, all back two-thirds."

In the control room two decks below, the helmsman turned the wheel, setting the rudder as directed. At the maneuvering station, the men manning the steam throttles at the propulsion panel received the all back two-thirds order. They opened the throttle, and steam poured into the main turbines. The turbines drive the twin propellers of the submarine, through reduction gears. With a long blast of the foghorn, the *Nautilus* signaled that she was under way.

Nearby stood the escort vessel the *Skylark*, her decks crammed with naval observers and newsmen. They watched the dark gray shadow move away from the dock, backing slowly through the shallow waters into the main channel.

But just before she was to turn around to head south, the chief engineer reported to Commander Wilkinson, "There's a rubbing sound in the starboard shaft."

This was unfortunate, for it could mean trouble in one of the two main turbines or in the intricate gearbox that conveyed power from the turbine to the starboard propeller. And it was particularly bad at this moment because the plan was to swing the stern to the left before making the turn to go forward. Wilkinson ordered the starboard turbine shut down and the shaft switched to what is called "reactor creep," in which the propeller is operated by electric power drawn from a generator driven by the reactor, instead of by the steam-powered turbine. This meant only a fraction of the power, however.

Unable to stand the suspense up on the bridge,

hearing only relayed reports on the problem, Rickover, his Navy raincoat flying, hurried below. The *Nautilus* still crept forward, limping on one turbine and faced with a choppy sea as she negotiated the turn.

Although Wilkinson had planned to send the message "Under way 1100 Roger, on nuclear power," he refrained, fearing that the problem might mean coming back to the dock. Instead, he flashed "Under way from Electric Boat Division," as he moved slowly into the Long Island Sound.

Below, the engineers tested the reduction gear to determine the cause of the unearthly screeching noise. By working with it, they found that they could work the turbine if in the ahead position, and so progressed that way.

As they passed the U.S.S. *Skylark*, the historic message was readied. Then, for the first time, a Naval vessel reported "Under way on nuclear power."

The *Nautilus* continued out into open water, checking propeller shaft vibrations, cruising up and down while the technicians made measurements and the crew got the feel of the ship. The seas were quite high, the winds brisk, and ice formed on the deck as the *Nautilus* headed out for open sea. Test after test was conducted nonetheless, the crew elated because of the responsiveness of the ship.

While some damage was sustained by the *Nautilus*, minor dents and ripped-up deck planking, the captain reported there were more complaints of seasickness than anything else. Since the *Nautilus* was taking the sea on her beam for the tests, the motion was much worse than it would have been otherwise. When a few of the crew suggested to Rickover that the tests be halted for a while because of the heavy sea, they got only a baleful glare in return.

There were a few oil and water leaks and two electrical fires which were rapidly extinguished on the *Nautilus'* first voyage. But Wilkinson, veteran of five such shakedown cruises, reported far less trouble than the average newly constructed vessel. All the problems were conventional, and there was no trouble at all with the nuclear reactor. The worrisome mechanical problem which had resulted in their cautious takeoff was found to be very minor, just a screw which had worked loose and was rubbing on the reduction gear.

Three days later the *Nautilus* again departed from the Electric Boat Division dock on its second builder's trial cruise, this time with an even more ambitious schedule. Without hesitation this time, and considerably faster, she backed around and headed toward Montauk Point, Long Island. Again the submarine escort *Skylark* stood by, this time shipping 12-foot waves as she waited for *Nautilus* to prepare for diving tests. This was indeed a crucial test; any error in construction would make itself all too evident in the increasing high pressure as she penetrated deeper into the sea. The test was to be longer this time, the crew remaining submerged for a week. Although tests had been run to see how the men would react to it, this would be the first time they had actually been in an operational situation, confined beneath the sea with a live nuclear reactor. And while the *Nautilus* reactor was considered quite safe from radiation leaks, having been tested thoroughly under many conditions of stress, the radiation patches worn by the crew would be monitored carefully.

In the early afternoon of January 20, out in the international waters off the New York coast, the boat was slowed down until it was barely moving. All the sea valves and hatches were closed and the ship was checked to see if it was tight. The ballast tanks were opened, and the bow and stern planes tilted to bring her down.

"Fire," one of the crew exclaimed. Another crewman leaped instantly to break an electrical circuit near the wire which had shorted, producing a flash of fire, and as quickly as it had come it was out.

A few instants later there was another electrical fire caused by a short circuit in the control panel for the submarine's snorkel. Another quick reaction by the crew extinguished the flame.

Then as the sub submerged completely—a feat which took only seven minutes from the order to dive—a number of small leaks were detected. These were soon fixed in the routine operation of tightening packing glands around valves where the leaks occurred.

The *Nautilus* moved up and down in the water for the next hour, the crew finding that she responded rapidly with the new single-stick controls. She ran at around 100 feet for about a half hour, then signaled to the *Skylark* that she was coming back up. Using high-pressure air to blow the water out of her ballast tanks, she rose to periscope depth, then slowly surfaced.

The *Nautilus* made almost fifty dives during this second trial run, and according to Captain Wikinson, the forty-first dive was made with an old submariner at the helm. Wilkinson reported later that Admiral Hyman Rickover completed his dive in 52 seconds, but then played a joke on the captain. As he completed his dive, he whimsically gave orders for the boat to be taken down and put on the bottom, all ahead full, take charge Captain Wilkinson. The captain of course had to hastily countermand these orders. Wilkinson also reported that during this voyage, a happy-birthday message from the *Nautilus* at sea was sent to Mrs. H. G. Rickover in Washington, D.C.

According to reports, the dives were made in comparatively shallow water from about 100 to 150 feet, off Long Island. As to the radiation received by the men during this time, the average was about 45 millirads. The Atomic Energy Commission's experts at that time said that 300 millirads a week would not be harmful, so the men were exposed to a negligible amount.

The *Nautilus* was brought back to Groton for routine maintenance, which took about a month. Then she steamed back out to sea, now farther out into the Atlantic than before, for even more rigorous and deeper dives. These took precise calculations by the diving officer, who determined exactly how many pounds of water had to be flooded into the ballast tanks. As the depth changed, the pressure and temperature of the water changed, thus making the amount that had to be taken on to dive different at each depth. Although the depths of these dives were classified, there were some speculations that the *Nautilus* reached as deep as 1,000 feet, some 300 feet below the record depth of a conventional submarine.

Congress was intensely interested in these performances, and those associated with the *Nautilus* decided it was about time they showed her off a little. An invitation was extended to the Joint Committee on Atomic Energy to make a visit, and it was decided that the committee would hold its next meeting submerged in the nuclear submarine. The date set was March 20, 1955.

At 11 o'clock that night, a dozen Senators and Representatives of the Congress of the United States of America filed on the dock and were handed the standard radiation badge to pin on their lapels. The crew was understandably nervous at this assemblage, and one young officer produced a chuckle from everyone as he confusedly introduced himself to Senator Bourke Hickenlooper as "Lieutenant Hickenlooper, sir."

The lawmakers were surprised by the comfort they found aboard the *Nautilus*. Its streamlined bulkheads were painted a soothing combination of browns and greens. A jukebox, playing six records for a nickel, broadcast music which could be heard all over the boat, thanks to the absence of noisy diesel engines. The lack of bulky batteries and diesel engines also permitted more room for amenities for the crew, including a galley always open for snacks for men coming off a shift, and a comfortable mess hall which converted to a movie theater or television viewing room. The sub also boasted the only submerged Coca-Cola machine.

After a resplendent meal of automatically cooked turkey, the committee came to order. The diving klaxon suddenly blared, and the officer on the loud-speaker shouted, "Clear the bridge. Dive! Dive!" The lawmakers adjusted themselves in their seats, bracing for an expected shock. But the submarine tilted only slightly, and they soon relaxed.

In the excitement of the moment, they began to joke.

"I guess we have to call this a 'sub' committee," one said. Later another said with pained laughter, "I hope this isn't slanted testimony," when the vessel went into a sharp undersea turn.

Yet they were seriously aware of the implications of what they were seeing. They knew the limitations of the conventional submarines which made them the ultimate victim of the stalking destroyer, who had but to wait until the submarine's batteries ran out. The *Nautilus* could cruise on indefinitely, speeding faster underwater than the surface ships could on the surface. And as an attack submarine, she would still be going strong when the destroyer had to refuel.

Knowing the value of good public relations, the Navy arranged a treat for the Congressmen. As they met in the officer's wardroom that night, new records for speed and depth were announced for the sub-marine.

Members of the joint committee were ebullient and

more than a little smug when they returned to tell about their adventure to their colleagues. Praise of the sub, Captain Wilkinson, and Admiral Rickover was heard in both the House and the Senate. "The atomic submarine will be the capital ship of the Navy of the future. It seems to be self-evident that a decade from now the conventional submarine will be replaced almost entirely by atomic submarines. It seems to be self-evident in addition that our Soviet rivals will do everything in their power to best us in the struggle for underwater supremacy—which means supremacy in atomic subs," one member told the Senate.

Senator Clinton P. Anderson, Democrat from New Mexico, entered a new thought. "It strikes me as ironical that a vessel of this type, equipped with a revolutionary atomic power plant, should be armed with conventional torpedoes little improved over the torpedoes of World War Two. An atomic submarine must have atomic armaments."

There were a few in the Navy who were struck by the same idea. Rear Admiral William F. Raborn and his staff had watched with a great deal of interest the development of the nuclear submarine. They saw its potential as a mobile missile-launching base, lurking off the enemy's coastlines, camping in the deep cold waters where even sonar devices could not detect it.

The use of the nuclear submarine would answer the criticisms of other missile defenses. The intercontinental ballistic missile (ICBM) was peculiarly vulnerable to a bombing attack as it was raised high above the ground before launching. (Later the Air Force

125

would develop means to protect the missiles in hardened silos beneath the ground.) The intermediate range ballistic missiles (IRBM) of the Army, because of their limited range, had to be positioned on foreign soil to be within striking range of a potential enemy. Yet in the depths of the world's oceans, covering almost 70 percent of the globe, there would be almost no chance of sabotage, no need for involved treaties with foreign governments.

Raborn's idea was to marry a solid propellant missile—considered safer than the volatile and highly flammable liquid propellants for shipboard use and definitely smaller, because the fuel itself is the motor —to an atomic warhead. Then he thought to put this devastating weapon on the nuclear submarine.

The technological problems looked staggering. First, no solid rocket fuel then in existence had the specific impulse, or potential thrusting power per pound, to meet the Navy's requirement. Then there was the problem of launching the rocket up through many fathoms of water without having it wobble or change course because of the pressure of the water. And if the submarine were not exactly level, how could they be sure the missile was headed in the right direction?

If it could be done, Admiral "Red" Raborn was determined he would be the one to do it. An old pilot, he had the "seat of the pants" knack of making instant decisions in a manner so decisive and so often right that he amazed those around him. His tactics and personality were a contrast to Rickover. Red used persuasion at its best, smiling while he probed to get the best work out of his men.

Raborn, not an engineer, was an engaging man who could sell his audience on almost any idea he had if he put his heart into it. As an administrator and project leader, he was strict and to the point. Both he and Rickover had the highest personal standards and set exhausting examples at their jobs for their staffs to live up to. Both believed in personal contact with the industry and field elements of their projects, traveling days to see for themselves how the work was going on. Both got results in projects other men had termed impossible.

Raborn also was an Annapolis graduate, but he became a carrier pilot who flew many a combat mission against the Japanese in World War II. His experience was in development of tactical air-launched missiles after the war, and for his leadership in this program he was chosen to head the new project.

When he was informed of his new post, he knew there was by no means an atmosphere of general acceptance in the Defense Department. There were interservice rivalries and a widespread belief that the job was impossible. But Navy Secretary Charles Thomas and Chief of Naval Operations Arleigh Burke believed in it and created a separate office, called the Special Projects Office, with Raborn at its head.

Raborn was given a great deal of authority, having to report only to the Secretary of the Navy. He also received a "hunting license" in a letter from Thomas and Burke, which said that they were to be notified personally if any difficulty was encountered, and anything which might slow down the project was to be taken immediately to the highest level without going through the usual, time-consuming channels.

For his staff, he was told that he could draw upon the expertise of the Navy, calling on the best technical experts and managers he could find. Yet, all was not as perfect as it may have sounded. Raborn also knew that funds were in short supply, and that the top-priority label attached to his project did not necessarily mean that it would take precedence over the jealously guarded developments of the other services, and indeed, over such projects as the nuclear submarine itself in the Navy.

In December, 1955, the staff of the nuclear submarine project got a new neighbor, as Raborn and his men quietly moved into two crowded rooms in the dilapidated "W" building where Rickover had been now for years. No ladies' room for him, but his quarters were just as crowded.

Thus, they set to work on their idea of the fleet ballistic missile, referred to as the FBM. At first, they were bogged down by an order by the Secretary of Defense to use the Army's liquid-fueled rocket, the Jupiter. But developments in solid fuels, in which the fuel and the oxidizer are already mixed and solidified like a giant candle, looked promising, and eventually they would switch. Another breakthrough would make the concept even more feasible. The Atomic Energy Commission would announce that it could make devastatingly powerful atomic warheads a frac-

128

tion of the size and weight they had previously been limited to. This would make it possible to carry a number of the deadly missiles on each nuclear submarine.

The missile would be named Polaris, after the sailor's oldest navigational friend, the North Star.

While Raborn's dream was taking its initial shape, the *Nautilus* continued to prove herself to the Navy. In May, 1955, she made a completely submerged shakedown cruise from New London, Connecticut, to San Juan, Puerto Rico, a distance of almost 1,400 miles, in less than 90 hours. Records for submerged speed, duration underwater, duration without the use of a snorkel, and total passage speed were set during this cruise, only to be broken in a successive voyage up the East Coast from Key West to New London.

But it was in "war games" with the fleet that her star shone. Out in the Atlantic, a great trap of Naval vessels, carriers, hunter-killer submarines, destroyers, and cruisers was set for the lone submarine. Each ship was equipped with the best the Navy had to offer in detection and antisubmarine warfare devices, sonar, radar, depth charges, magnetic instruments, and others still secret.

This was a crucial test. Could the *Nautilus* successfully evade the dozens of suspicious searchers with her quiet nuclear engines and her ability to stay submerged?

As the *Nautilus* glided along in the deep underwater, the sonar operator sat, his attention intensely trained to his earphones. The high-frequency supersonic waves emanating from his instruments bounced off every object for miles around—the ocean floor with its mountains and valleys, the schools of fish and sardines, old wrecks of boats from days gone by, and even from the *Nautilus* itself.

In all this racket, his job was to detect the other ships. The mechanically rhythmic chugging of their diesel engines and the sound of their propellers were relatively easy to identify. The *Nautilus'* own turbines are relatively quiet, discernible only from a few thousand yards. At depth her propellers are muffled. She can be identified only if a ship passing overhead happens to find her with an echo range, a sonar bounce or "ping."

The *Nautilus* played a mouse's game with the ships, darting in and out of the area where another submarine would have been detected sooner or later. She glided swiftly toward one, than another, daring them to find her. In the protocol of the war games, her crew chalked off their names as she "sank" them with hypothetical torpedoes.

Then the diving planes were set and the *Nautilus* moved even deeper, set on a new mission. Her job: to determine whether the atomic submarine can penetrate the country's coastline defenses and launch an offensive attack on one of its shoreline cities.

When she reached the prescribed depth, she slowed and her planes were once more changed to horizontal to keep her at the operational depth. The crew was alert, poised, and caught up in the simulation. In its way it was as important as a real mission; much had to be proved.

The navigator plotted the course around the known positions of the waiting ships above; the gyrocompass was set. The sonar operator, a fresh crew member who relieved the first man in this tedious job, listened to the sonar fathometer as it described to him the ocean landscape below.

All other sound was muffled as the boat moved near a group of ships. The skipper took the *Nautilus* around them and put her back on the course toward a large port city. Cautiously she moved toward this goal. The skipper used his weapons of speed and quiet to dodge the searching ships, planes, and submarines.

As she approached the Continental Shelf, she had to climb back into shallow water where the chances of detecting her propellers by sonar were much greater. But the skipper had an ace in the hole; he could mix her sounds with those of the noisy freighters moving in the shipping lanes. He adjusted her speed and depth to match one on its way to port, hitching an auditory ride in. Once within range, she surfaced undetected, staying long enough to complete the mock barrage of the cities nearby. She had accomplished her mission.

To many Navy men, the *Nautilus* had profoundly demonstrated that anything not nuclear was obsolete, as far as submarines went. The vessel had truly opened up the underwater for Navy operations. In effect, they said, the *Nautilus* was the first true submarine.

Up until that time, submarines had been designed with surface operations in mind. Their hulls were designed like surface ships, for greatest stability during the long hours while they recharged their batteries.

It had been known since the time of Archimedes that a different form, a spindle form, would permit the greatest speed for underwater operations. However, since the spindle-form boat was very difficult to handle on the surface, it had not been popular in submarine design. But with the *Nautilus* becoming a true creature of the deep, there was concern about her high speeds and the relationship between ship design and control. To get more information about the spindle configuration, the Navy designed a small diesel-powered submarine named the *Albacore.*

The bomb-shaped *Albacore,* with her potbelly and wide beam, looked awkward indeed as she chugged along on the surface in trial cruises from the U.S. Naval base at Portsmouth, New Hampshire. She had a single propeller, and her lines were streamlined without the proturberances associated with previous submarine design. But when she dived she no longer was a crude misfit. She proved that the design could add as much as one-third to the speed of the boat. Even before the actual underseas tests, the engineers were fairly certain of this result, for the bomb shape had been tested in wind tunnels, like an airplane, to determine its performance as it moved swiftly through a fluid. Since air also is a fluid, although hundreds of times less dense than water, the test was valid.

In December, 1955, the Navy decided to design a new submarine class using nuclear propulsion with the *Albacore*-type hull. The group would be called the Skipjack class and would be nuclear fast-attack submarines. They would be the most rapid submarines in existence and would operate almost exclusively underwater.

But there was an ironic note in all this. Although the *Nautilus* had proven herself so beautifully, she apparently had not convinced everyone. In requesting funds for the new fiscal year, the Navy ordered a new conventionally powered diesel-electric submarine.

9

A Sudden Awakening

The first people to get the idea of launching missiles from submarines were the Germans, who toyed with the idea during World War II. Luckily for the world, perhaps, the development work on the V-2 rocket, headed by German Army General Walter R. Dornberger and his technical management director, Dr. Wernher von Braun, was not far enough along to permit their actual use before the end of the war.

The man to whom the idea is credited was named Ernst Steinhoff, an engineer working with Von Braun at Peenemünde, the German rocket development base on the Baltic Sea. He had a brother, Fritz Steinhoff, who was a U-boat commander. Fritz told Ernst about the limitations of the submarines arsenal, with its few torpedoes, and how he had wished he had had some of the V-2 rockets on a recent mission off the Casablanca coast, where he had observed a huge mobilization of Allied ships, men, and supplies unloading in the harbor. A few rockets would have wiped out the entire convoy, he said, and the submarine probably could have escaped.

The two brothers approached Von Braun with the idea, which attracted his immediate interest. Together they rigged up an experiment. Fritz managed to get an old submarine for the test, while some of the men at Peenemünde worked on the adaption of some rocket racks for a launching structure. Some artillery rockets were waterproofed with candle wax, and a wire igniter was rigged up.

The submarine was taken to a depth of about 75 feet with the three men aboard. The rockets were ignited, and one by one, in the hushed silence, they streaked away from the submarine for the surface. Moving picture cameras posted on the nearby shore caught them as they popped cleanly out of the water, traveled for a short distance, and finally dropped.

When Dornberger was shown the results, he was enthused. The group began looking for the best means of mounting the rockets. However, technical difficulties and the end of the war prevented their going any further with the idea.

The rocket experts headed by the young Von Braun were eagerly sought by every Allied country as the war ended. The Russians were particularly interested in getting this top scientific talent, for purposes which would be revealed only later. A few forward-thinking U.S. Army Intelligence officers, led by Colonel Holger N. Toftoy, appreciated the value of having in the United States this team of experts who had brought rocketry to a point never achieved by any other nation.

Toftoy managed to persuade his superiors in Washington that an effort should be made to get as many of the top management and technical men from the rocket base as possible. Toftoy requested permission to bring over three hundred, but the administration, facing a high level of public resentment toward any Germans, told him to limit the number to one hundred.

Together with Von Braun, Toftoy interviewed all the men who said they would like to go to the United States. Finding recruits was no problem, for almost all the members of Von Braun's close-knit group, including Wernher himself, had decided long ago that they would cast their lot with the Americans in preference to the Russians or any of the other countries who had evidenced interest in capturing them. In fact, it had been they themselves who had, as the end of the war approached and its outcome became obvious, arranged to wait in a region where they knew they were closest to American troops.

A total of 115 men were chosen, all of whom Von Braun deemed essential in building a new development operation. They numbered among them laboratory chiefs, managers, and even a communications expert as well as scientists.

Together with a number of captured V-2 rockets, the Germans were taken to Fort Bliss, Texas, where they began once again launching test rockets, at the White Sands Army Proving Ground. Here they were visited by members of all the services, including Navy men who listened with awe at the admission from Von Braun that the Germans had tried to launch rockets from submarines.

After a few tests, one in which a liquid-fueled V-2 was launched and purposely exploded on a simulated ship deck, the idea was shelved for a few years. This ship-deck explosion scared the spunk out of some of the officers who thought rockets were a good idea.

When Admiral Raborn set about the task of developing the fleet ballistic missile, he remembered the dangers of liquid-propelled rockets and sought to develop a solid-fueled rocket instead. Thus, while the Navy owed its original idea to the Germans, it soon set off on its own course.

The Polaris missile was to be 28 feet long and weigh about 28,000 pounds. Sixteen missiles could be carried inside a nuclear submarine, one considerably larger than the *Nautilus*. The power plant would be created by Rickover's Naval reactors group.

One of Raborn's greatest talents was the ability to pick the best people for each job. "If you can't get the best man, then get his advice," was his motto.

For Polaris' propulsion system, he enlisted the services of the Aerojet-General Company, a division of General Tire and Rubber Company. The Aerojet people worked on a number of mixtures of chemicals, fuels, and oxidizers before they found one which had a high specific impulse or energy-generating power, and which would not explode at the slightest jarring. To be sure, there were several costly accidents before the proper formula was achieved, but eventually it was.

The mixture of chemicals was poured into huge molds which would permit it to set in cylindrical cones with an open, star-shaped core running through the center. The shape was important, for it had much effect on the burning characteristics of the motor. Nozzles with movable vanes in them directed the exhaust, and thus the direction of the missile itself.

The navigation system used by all the nuclear submarines was called the ships inertial navigation system, or SINS for short. This system was the answer to the special problem of the nuclear submarine: with its capability of remaining submerged for weeks on end, it would not have the stars and sun for reference in determining its position.

Dr. Charles Stark Draper of the Massachusetts Institute of Technology became known as the Father of Inertial Guidance for his development of the SINS. The heart of the navigation system, as it had also been in the V-1 and V-2 missiles developed by the Germans, was a gyroscope.

Movements of the ship were sensed by accelerometers, which measured any motion by the effect it had on small weights attached to springs. This information was fed into the computer, which would tell exactly what position the ship was in at the time. Each nuclear submarine was to have three SINS units to ensure complete accuracy and enough extra equipment so that if one ceased to function during a long voyage, the others would still be available.

The SINS system development was watched closely by Raborn, as was the development of the fire control system, which had to have lightning-quick reflexes in giving target signals to each of the Polaris missiles inside the submarine.

The management technique developed by Raborn to keep track of all the complex systems which had to be brought together in the development of the Polaris system has been considered one of the best accomplishments on the new era of technology.

The program evaluation and review technique, or PERT as it has become known, is what would seem to be simple common sense. However, like many other extremely good developments, simplicity was arrived at only after much research. This research was done by a management expert named Gordon Pehrson, who sought to grant his boss, Raborn, his wish that he would be able to reach down to any level of Special Projects activity and find out exactly what was going on and how it affected the total system development.

After reviewing the management techniques developed in a myriad of companies in different fields, Pehrson realized he would have to develop his own plan. What he came up with was a system of charts, constantly updated, which showed the exact developmental status of all the various aspects, propulsion, navigation, fire control, and the like. Graphs illustrated the progress of each particular part in a system. Various colored markers flagged the condition it was in: blue meant ahead of schedule; red, behind; green, exactly on schedule; and orange, uncertain. Raborn could pinpoint trouble areas at a glance and direct his attention accordingly.

Contractors also were put on deadlines and told to

report regularly on how they were meeting milestone events toward the deadlines. A special management center was constructed to house these tools, and it became the nerve center of the project.

The extremely precise management control over every part of the program was probably the deciding factor in Raborn's success in responding to the call of the administration when some unexpected events changed America's outlook on a great many things.

The submarine missile program got its first real impetus with the report of a secret Presidential committee headed by the president of the Massachusetts Institute of Technology, Dr. James R. Killian. This committee was assembled in 1954 to survey the relative military strengths of the United States and Russia.

The Killian committee reported that the Soviet Union, having recently exploded its own hydrogen bomb, was rapidly gaining on the United States in military power. It recommended development of several rocket programs, one of which was the Navy's fleet ballistic missile program.

As the months wore on, there were further evidences of the Soviet Union's intentions. The cold war intensified with the suppression of the Hungarian uprising. Yet no one was really prepared for what was soon to happen.

During 1956, scientists returning from international meetings reported that Soviet Union representatives were giving strong hints that they planned to launch an artificial earth satellite. Both the United States and the Soviet Union, in conjunction with the celebration of the International Geophysical Year, had talked about the benefits of such satellites for scientific exploration outside the earth's atmosphere. (The IGY was a period from July, 1957, to December, 1958, set by scientists for cooperative study throughout the world on the activities of the sun, which would be at its peak of an eleven-year sunspot cycle. At this time, it would send out more radiation than at any other time during the cycle.)

Yet there were few who really believed that the Soviet Union had the technological knowledge to launch a satellite. Hadn't the United States been the leading scientific power for many decades, as confirmed once again by her achievement in attaining nuclear fission?

When at these meetings the Russian scientists made vague references to their plans to launch satellites, the American scientists smiled smugly. The Americans had their own project, a Navy satellite to be launched by a Vanguard rocket. That the rocket was untested and had real technical problems bothered them not a bit; U.S. technology would prevail, they were sure.

They were wrong, as history all too well informs us. On October 4, 1957, at a reception in the Soviet embassy in Washington, D.C., official Washington was given the news that the Soviets, in launching a 184-pound satellite in earth orbit, had done what the United States could not do.

The effect on American morale was devastating. While the general public discussed in some fear the possible consequences of the action, the top military planners locked themselves in their offices to evaluate the situation and decide what they should recommend to the President. Although President Eisenhower took the official position that the Soviet satellite was not of any importance militarily, other administration officials were shaken badly.

Military intelligence knew that the Soviets had fired an intercontinental ballistic missile (ICBM) with a dummy warhead some thousands of miles down a test range just a few weeks before. The threat to the United States was growing: she was within striking range of the enemy, even though that enemy was halfway across the world. Sputnik emphasized the Soviet Union's rocket capability, and there was the fear that she would place bombs in orbit which could be dropped on the United States at a moment's notice.

Although the United States had brought the top German rocket experts to America after the war, it had not exploited this prize. Instead, it had given the Germans a few rockets to launch in high-altitude research, and just enough work to keep them occupied. Von Braun and his men chafed at the relaxed pace; they sensed what was going on in the Soviet Union.

The Soviets, out of a sense of inferiority, had embarked on a crash program immediately after the war to develop a big rocket. The United States so conclusively had the upper hand with the world's first atomic bomb that the Russians sought for some means to counter this advantage.

They settled on rockets as the best means of carrying huge amounts of explosives, and later the heavy, crude atomic warheads they at first developed.

The American atomic bomb, by comparison, was a sophisticated device which could be carried in an airplane.

Thus, as the United States conducted leisurely launches at White Sands, out of curiosity more than anything else, the Soviets perfected their tools for the day they would launch the first artificial satellite and command the attention of the world. This they did, the satellite itself being only symbolic of the great technological effort under way in Russia which presented a threat on all fronts.

The Defense Department immediately called on each project office to draw up a plan outlining how it could respond to the Soviet threat. When Sputnik II, weighing 1,120 pounds and carrying a live dog, went into orbit, the pressure for action increased.

When the call came to Raborn's Special Projects Office, he turned his full attention to the problem. With adequate funds, he determined, several years might be shaved off the 1963 deadline for the Polaris missile development time. However, it would require cutting the range of the missile from 1,500 to 1,200 miles. If the Pentagon would accept this imposition, Raborn said, the Special Projects Office would deliver the missile in 1960.

The decision involved not only the missile but the nuclear submarine as well. It had been planned to build a larger submarine especially for the Polaris concurrently with the missile. The new schedule allowed no such luxury; in fact, the time left was too short to build the submarine at all!

All the first submarines, beginning with the *Nau-*

tilus and *Seawolf,* had been attack submarines. Several had been built by the Electric Boat Division of General Dynamics, at Groton, Connecticut. Here also the first of the new Skipjack-class nuclear submarines was being built. This was the one in which the new hull design, proven out by the *Albacore*, was incorporated.

On the building ways at the time Sputnik first made its appearance in the sky was a submarine of the Skipjack class which was to be named the *Scorpion.* Her keel, already laid, measured 252 feet. Many of the steel hull sections were in place, and the items which had to be ordered in advance, such as turbine equipment, were in the works. Rickover's group already was developing the nuclear reactor.

The decision was made to stretch the *Scorpion,* cut it in half, and put in a new midsection containing additional control and navigation equipment as well as the racks for the 16 Polaris missiles. Instead of 252 feet, she would measure 380 feet long, and have a surface displacement of 5,400 tons.

The question was: Could the power plant provide the necessary power for this overgrown submarine? Rickover was called in and the question put to him. After considerable study, he arrived at the conclusion that the nuclear reactor already under development would be sufficient to power the new sub, although it might result in a slightly reduced speed.

The submarine was redesignated the *George Washington*, starting a tradition of naming the Polaris submarines after important figures in American history. A second hull also was designated for conversion to a Polaris submarine, and the Electric Boat Division went on a three-shift, twenty-four-hour day. Third and fourth duplications of the stretched *George Washington* were ordered from two other shipyards.

Rickover was often questioned as to what he thought about the Soviet satellite and what danger the country might be in. "The Russian submarines are presently a lot greater threat to us than the Sputniks are," he said.

In a national newsmagazine interview, Rickover said that the great danger lay in the fact that the United States didn't seem to know how to exploit developments as fast as the Russians. And he also pointed out that while the United States had the same basic knowledge on rockets, it failed to exploit it. Finally it was put in the position that even when it did attempt to put up a satellite, it couldn't match the payload put up by the Russians.

Sputnik is a psychological proposition, he said. By itself, it did not mean so much. But it could mean a great deal to the United States if it accepted it as a warning to improve its schools and to examine the system to see why it took so long to exploit technological developments.

In a speech made to the American Legion just a few weeks after the launch of the Soviet satellite, Rickover likened the Polaris missile submarine to an underwater satellite.

"These underwater satellites will launch their attack from far out in the Atlantic, the Pacific, or the Arctic Ocean. They could be placed anywhere within fifteen hundred miles of their targets. They could be dispersed over literally millions of square miles of ocean," he said.

To an audience of veterans who had their faith but not their patriotism shaken by the recent events, Rickover's words were soothing indeed.

They took heart in his message: "The underwater satellite marks the closest approach now foreseeable to the ideal mobile platform. It could go anywhere at any time. It could remain well hidden from the enemy. It would draw the enemy's missiles and bombs away from our cities and factories and farms, and draw them toward the uninhabited seas.

"The problem of locating and destroying such an underseas fleet will be tremendous. Search radar will be helpless against it. The enemy would be in the position of a man trying to find a black cat on a vast and empty plain on a moonless and starless night."

He warned that the Soviet navy was the second largest in the world, that the Soviet submarine fleet numbered about 500 to the American 110. Although there was no evidence that the Soviets had nuclear submarines, the day when they probably would was near. "The Soviets now have the capability of launching, from their submarines, missiles with a range of at least two hundred miles—presumably with nuclear warheads. It would take but a single such missile, accurately placed, to cripple any of our seaboard cities."

He stressed the importance of the attack submarines. "Clearly, the task of containing the Soviet submarine menace in the event of war would be formidable. In fact, this is the Navy's most vital and most difficult defensive mission.

"The heart of the problem would be to destroy the enemy's submarines in or close to their home bases—before they reached the open seas, if possible."

Air strikes by nuclear carrier forces might destroy the enemy's submarine bases, Rickover conjectured. "But we must assume that some of his ships would survive initial attacks and break out into the open seas.

"We are now developing a nuclear-powered submarine specifically to cope with this threat. We are also designing a nuclear power plant for another type of ship which will be very important for antisubmarine warfare, a frigate. We hope to be able to start construction of this frigate in the near future. It will be needed to protect our naval task forces against submarine attack.

"The nuclear task force will be unlike its closely knit counterpart of World War Two," he said. "In order to reduce vulnerability to hydrogen bomb attack, the nuclear task force will be dispersed over an area as big as the state of New York. No ship will be within H-bomb radius of another."

Rickover noted that the mere existence of the underseas fleet would create a tremendous problem for an aggressor. Although it might know the location of the fixed land-based missile sites and calculate that it could destroy most of the land-based force in a surprise attack, it could not make any rational calculation for an attack against hidden and mobile underwater satellites. It might take a number of missiles just to destroy one submerged launching platform.

"I should make it plain that this weapon cannot be built by the day after tomorrow. It will be a scientific and engineering challenge, comparable in difficulty and magnitude to the first nuclear submarine," he warned.

"In other words, the *Nautilus* did not mark the end of a technological road. It marked the beginning. It should be compared with the first airplane that flew at Kitty Hawk. For every problem we have already solved in the short history of nuclear power, a hundred problems remain to be solved," he stressed.

But the nuclear Navy was indeed taking shape. The *Seawolf,* the second nuclear attack submarine and the one with a sodium-cooled reactor, was launched in 1955, the *Skate* in spring of 1957, and the *Swordfish* and the *Sargo* soon afterward. The Navy soon made a significant decision: it would build no more diesel submarines except for the three then under construction.

The *Nautilus,* after thousands of miles of travel, finally ran out of nuclear fuel, and a new core had to be installed. The submarine ran 62,500 miles, 37,000 of them fully submerged, on the first core. The new core would last even longer.

For comparison, Rickover told Congress, a conventional submarine running that distance would have consumed 2,170,000 gallons of oil, the amount contained in 217 tank cars stretching 1.7 miles long. Obviously, one submarine could not hold all this oil at one time; thus she would have had to make many refueling stops. The nuclear fuel was not cheaper yet, but it gave to the fleet a profound military advantage.

The Navy also was building a larger submarine, to be powered by a two-reactor power plant. The submarine, named the *Triton,* was to be a radar picket, which would be used to picket fleet stations in a circle and warn against impending air attack. She would be the largest submarine ever constructed, with an overall length of 447½ feet, and the first to be powered by twin reactors.

The reactors were being built by the General Electric Company at West Milton, New York, under Rickover's direction. Electric Boat Division once again was working on the submarine itself.

Rickover told Congress that he considered the development of the two-reactor submarine one of the most important items in a vast program under way for changing the Navy. "Its propulsion plant can also be used for large submarines carrying ballistic missiles. In fact, we had this in mind from the very first. It was changed over from the original concept of a missile-carrying submarine to a radar picket sub," he said.

The nuclear aircraft carrier project, which for a while had been relegated to the Shippingport form only, was revived around 1956, and funds were appropriated to start manufacture of its equipment.

The Naval reactors division design called for eight reactors, two reactors per shaft. It also would have an auxiliary power plant which would use more power than the main propulsion plants of the battleships of the last war. The plan was to build one such nuclear carrier each year, starting with the 1958 shipbuilding program.

Also under way was the design of a guided missile cruiser, the first of which would be named the *Long Beach.* This ship would displace 14,000 tons and have the same type of reactor as the aircraft carrier, except that it would have only two of them.

Rickover also had working a plan for a new frigate prototype which he was not yet ready to ask for development money for.

They had learned a great deal in the past few years and accomplished much. One important technical discovery was the fact that the sodium-cooled submarine intermediate reactor, as employed in the *Seawolf,* was simply not as efficient as the water-cooled reactor like the *Nautilus'.* Sodium was found to become 30,000 times as radioactive as water, and the dangers of leaks became much greater. Maintenance was very costly. For this reason, *Seawolf* was taken out of the fleet, her reactor was removed and retired, and a water-cooled reactor was installed.

Rickover was not disappointed, however, and stressed the importance of following alternate approaches to each problem. He recommended working on even more than two types of reactors at a time, saying he thought this worthwhile "considering the fact that we are going to be spending many millions of dollars on these ships."

A great accomplishment of the program had been the development of new industries, such as a zirconium industry not even dreamed about before the development of nuclear reactors.

But the most far-reaching accomplishments were in the nuclear submarine field. As the attack submarine force and the promise of Polaris gave back to the United States a sense of security, the *Nautilus* gave it back a heaping measure of pride by becoming the first vessel to pass under the North Pole, on August 3, 1958.

10

Honors

The East Room of the White House was crowded. Rows upon rows of navy-blue uniforms, sporting gold braid, proclaimed the presence of the Navy's hierarchy. On the other side of the room were the muted tones of the civilian bureaucrats, the grays and blues slightly rumpled in the August heat. The sun glared in brightly, casting shining reflections on the gold and white decorations and breaking into color in the crystal chandeliers.

There was a sense of elation among all present. The occasion was one of triumph for the Navy. President Dwight D. Eisenhower had called the commander of the *Nautilus,* William R. Anderson, for the purpose of honoring him for guiding the *Nautilus* in its historic voyage under the North Pole.

The room was crowded with newspapermen and photographers as the President strode into the room, his face beaming. He beckoned the photographers closer as he signaled Commander Anderson to come forward.

As Eisenhower took his place behind the blue podium emblazoned with the Presidential seal, the questions began circulating in whispers among the newsmen. "What's it all about?" asked one in an undertone.

"Something to do with a nuclear sub," said another.

The newsmen then turned their critical eyes upon the room, identifying one dignitary after another, making notes and marking questions for possible interviews later. There they saw the Secretary of Defense, the Secretary of the Navy, the Chief of Naval Operations, and other top officials.

"The brass really turned out for this one," one of the reporters muttered, signaling to his photographer to capture some of the famous faces on film.

At a signal from the president, the room became silent. With a pleased grin, Eisenhower announced to the world that the *Nautilus* had crossed the North Pole.

Flashbulbs began popping as the President turned to Anderson. To the *Nautilus* crew, he said, he was awarding the first Presidential Unit Citation ever conferred on a unit in peacetime.

The Legion of Merit he presented to Commander Anderson. He read the citation: "To Commander Anderson, who by foresighted planning, skilled seamanship, and thorough study of the Arctic area, succeeded in cruising the *Nautilus* across the top of the world from the Bering Sea to the Greenland Sea, passing submerged beneath the geographic North Pole.

"Under his intrepid leadership," Eisenhower read, "*Nautilus* pioneered a submerged sea lane between the Eastern and Western hemispheres. This points the way for further exploration and possible use of this route by nuclear-powered cargo submarines as a new commercial between the major oceans of the world."

To a standing ovation, he pinned the medal on the commander.

At this, most of the reporters ran out of the room to the press room telephones, eager to tell the story of the *Nautilus* feat. A few, however, remained, scanning the room, searching for a particular face.

"I get the feeling something's missing," one said to another.

"You're right. It's Rickover," said the other.

They stopped a White House aide. "Where's Admiral Rickover?"

"Well," he said with an embarrassed shrug, "the Navy made up the list."

Hot on the trail of a story, the reporters cornered a Navy information officer, who passed the buck back to the White House.

The President's press secretary supplied the answer. Rickover just hadn't been invited.

"Wasn't invited? Why, he built the thing, didn't he?" the reporters asked incredulously.

"Well, yes," was the answer. "But there wasn't enough room for everyone, and the Navy officers were asked on the basis of rank, and only top-ranking heads of departments made it."

Commander Anderson, who had been whisked by

155

helicopter off the *Nautilus* when it surfaced off the coast of Ireland and then brought by Navy transport plane directly to the White House, was unaware at first that Rickover was not present.

When he found out, however, he was deeply disturbed. As soon as the ceremonies at the White House were finished, he went directly to the Navy building to pay his respects to the admiral.

Once again Rickover found himself the subject of heated debate on the news pages, in Congress, and in the Pentagon and Navy building. Senator Clinton P. Anderson protested strongly against the snub.

"He probably wasn't invited because of the limitations in space in the Navy for a man who is and has been outspoken in his criticism of the old, outmoded Navy concepts," he said scornfully.

Congressmen pressed the Defense Department for an offical explanation of the incident.

The Secretary of the Navy, Thomas S. Gates, publicly apologized for the failure to invite Rickover to the ceremony. He admitted that the nomination of Navy officials to the award ceremony was made by the Navy.

The reason Rickover was not present, he attempted to explain, was an oversight. He was overlooked "in our preoccupation with the operational significance of the *Nautilus'* polar cruise." He admitted that the admiral's "devotion and scientific skill uniquely contributed to the creation of the ship."

Why was he overlooked?

The Associated Press capsulized Rickover's career by saying: "He rocked the boat." In doing so, it said,

"He embarrassed and chagrined Navy officials and made some of them mad enough to walk the plank.

"Many who know Rickover trace his troubles to his dogged determination to get a job done—no matter what. They say he doesn't care whose toes he steps on in his drive for nuclear-propelled ships for the fleet," the AP ticker said.

"He has defied protocol, blasted at conformity, pushed projects through over the heads of superior officers. Over the years, he has become a man apart in the tradition-bound Navy, a lone seawolf hard to know, and by many accounts, hard to work with."

Life magazine said: "Rickover is just about the prickliest personality in Washington today. Like the original Davy Crockett, he is 'clear meat ax disposition all the way through.' He does not believe in several fine old American household gods, such as the Team, the Thoughtful Suggestion, the Faith That Moves Mountains, Organization and Know How.

"The primary reason for Rickover's unpopularity, both among the high naval brass and the leaders of industry, is that he is not a Team or a System man. He is a red-tape cutter, a by-passer and a tromper-on-toes," the magazine said.

Stories were told of how Rickover "poked a long nose" into what contractors considered their own business. His critical eye and acid comments about any detail he felt was being mishandled were described.

His long working day and complete devotion to his job also were reported. *Life* told how "when he telephones an official of, say, the Electric Boat

Company in Groton, Connecticut, and says, 'Will you be in your office with all your people for a meeting at ten P.M. Saturday night?' he cannot understand why the idea is not enthusiastically received."

Senator Henry Jackson said, "He is a dissenter, a nonconformist in uniform. The man is a scientist and a genius. You would search hard and long to find a good scientist who is not a bit difficult. I was attracted to him ten years ago because he was like a breath of fresh air."

Rickover's co-workers described him as not so much a scientific genius as an outstanding engineer with mature technical judgment, whose best quality was the ability to anticipate trouble before it started.

The chief of the Naval Bureau of Ships said, "Rickover is a pretty tough guy to work with. He works like a dog himself, but he's not a happy, pleasant individual. People feel rebuffed by someone exceptionally tough and Rickover makes a fetish of that." The possibility that religious prejudice was involved was dismissed by the director of the Bureau of Ships. "The Navy has had other Jewish admirals," he pointed out. The Jewish Senator from New York, Jacob Javits, concurred. "It's more of a Billy Mitchell than a Dreyfus case," he said, referring to the Army general who fought the entire military establishment for the cause of air power.

The incident at the White House was not the only "oversight" to happen. According to *Life* magazine, Rickover had also not been included in the first list of dignitaries to be present at the formal dedication of the Shippingport atomic power plant the previous

May. Mrs. Rickover had never been asked to dedicate a nuclear submarine, although the honor had been conferred on a number of Congressmen's and Naval officers' wives.

Yet, in researching their stories, the reporters found that Rickover did have friends. "The closer one gets to Rickover the more warmth there appears to be: the handful of men who work intimately with him in his headquarters, if not sentimental about him, do have a reverence for him that borders on affection," one reporter wrote.

They found that he took good care of his men, helping them advance their careers as best he could. They turned up some little-known stories of great warmth: one man told of how, upon the death of one of his children, he received a call late in the night from Rickover, who had found an appropriate verse in the Bible which he thought might comfort him.

He had made some really good friends in Congress. His approach of complete candor and his outspoken views on whatever the Congressmen wanted to know refreshed and delighted the committees with which he dealt. It became a traditional thing each year with the Joint Committee on Atomic Energy, and then later with the Armed Services Committees of the House and Senate, to devote a couple of days to frank bull sessions with the admiral on whatever subject he cared to talk about.

Each year they asked him how the work was going, whether he had enough money, and whether anyone was raiding his organization or if there were any other troubles with which they could help him. Their attitude was far different from the usual confrontation between Congress and those who appeared before it to get approval for their budgets.

Several times when Rickover indicated he had not been given enough funding for a particular project, Congress itself intervened, adding funds, which it earmarked for his work alone, to the administration's request.

Throughout the new uproar, Rickover again kept silent, apparently irritated only because his work was being interrupted by the constant calls of reporters. "I'm too busy to worry about snubs," he told the Associated Press, who had asked him how he felt about not being asked to the White House.

"Forget the personal stuff," he told another reporter. "The real issue is what a man accomplishes."

His work was indeed bearing fruit. On August 10, Commander Anderson rejoined the *Nautilus* in England and headed it back out to sea. As he headed it west, logging another new record for the gallant submarine in crossing the Atlantic in six days, eleven hours, and fifty-five minutes. Average speed was 21 knots.

The *Skate,* third nuclear submarine and first of a new class with a slightly more advanced reactor than the *Nautilus,* set a new west-to-east submarine speed record across the Atlantic in her shakedown cruise. Crossing time was eight days and eleven hours. On the way back, she set another record.

Skate and *Seawolf* then participated in some submerged endurance tests, to see how well crew and machinery functioned for long periods of time while closed up and underwater. *Seawolf* held out for thirty days and five minutes, *Skate* managed one day longer. Just a few months later, *Seawolf* again submerged, this time for a sixty-day record.

Skate was chosen to follow the *Nautilus* under the polar ice pack. She was fitted out with cold-weather gear and special navigation equipment, and set out to sea on July 30, 1958. She approached the polar ice pack August 9, one day after the *Nautilus* reached the North Pole.

But the *Skate* had an additional mission, being charged with the task of determining whether a submarine could surface in the polynyas or openings in the ice.

With sensitive equipment, the crew found a crack in the ice large enough for the 268-foot-long submarine to surface through. Backing the submarine slowly into position, the crew prepared for the task of bringing her up into an area perhaps never before seen by man.

Inch by inch the submarine rose, until her sail cleared the surface. Her periscope was ordered up, revealing a breathtaking sight of white ice and blue water. As the lake was deemed large enough, the *Skate* was brought to the surface. The crew let out a cheer, the scientists scrambling up the ladder to get out on the ice to make measurements and take samples of water and ice.

After investigating the first polynya, the *Skate* again submerged and headed toward the North Pole. She surfaced through the ice a total of nine times, crossing the North Pole on August 12, 1958, and

161

visiting Station Alfa, an American scientific observation camp floating on an ice floe some 40 miles from the North Pole.

The *Skate* returned to the Arctic a few months later, after a shore leave in the United States. This time, in the first winter passage under the Arctic ice pack, she crashed her sail through at the North Pole, making March 17, 1959, an important date in Naval history. *Skate* proved conclusively that nuclear submarines could operate under the Arctic ice pack and surface through it any time of the year.

While at the North Pole, the crew held memorial services for the late Sir Hubert Wilkins, the submariner who had made twenty-four expeditions to the Arctic but had never reached the North Pole. According to his wish, his ashes were scattered at the Pole.

In that fall of 1958, the *Skate*'s sister ships, the *Swordfish* and the *Sargo*, also joined the fleet. The *Seadragon* would soon follow. On the building ways were *Skipjack, Scamp, Scorpion, Sculpin, Shark,* and *Snook*, the submarines which would incorporate the new *Albacore*-type hull. These subs would have diving planes mounted on the sail instead of on the bow, and a single propeller shaft running down the center.

All this hardly went unnoticed by Congress. On both sides of the political aisle, Democrat and Republican alike, a movement started to honor Admiral Rickover for his part in making these successes, which had brought so much honor to the United States, and to make up for the slight at the *Nautilus* ceremony.

They conferred in the cloakrooms off the Senate

chamber, discussing what could be done to demonstrate their appreciation. Their decision was to confer a singular honor on Rickover by presenting a special Congressional gold medal to him. A resolution providing for the medal was drafted and adopted unanimously.

Once again the question of Rickover's future was raised. Again he would be forced to retire in 1960 if he were not promoted. His Congressional supporters were aware of this and made their feelings known once again to the Pentagon.

To ensure that nothing would happen to embarrass the Navy, Secretary of the Navy Thomas Gates decided he'd better not leave the question of Rickover's promotion to another Navy selection board. Instead, he instructed his subordinates to arrange to have Rickover promoted to vice-admiral as soon as internal red tape could be worked out.

The move meant upgrading the position of director of the Naval reactors division, which Rickover already held, to a three-star or vice-admiral post. But this time there was no question about whether the job was one important to the Navy or not.

The White House had tried to make amends almost immediately after the *Nautilus* incident. President Eisenhower asked Rickover to be his personal representative in the New York welcoming ceremony for the *Nautilus* as she returned from her record-breaking trip across the Atlantic.

With Rickover aboard, the *Nautilus* steamed up the New York harbor, flanked by an honor escort of all the New York tugboats the harbor authority could muster. The admiral was a guest of honor of the mayor of New York in a ticker tape and brass band welcoming ceremony. Hundreds of thousands of people lined the streets and cheered as the Navy group drove slowly by in an open automobile cavalcade.

Back in Washington, the resolution to give Rickover a gold medal passed both Houses.

The joint Senate-House resolution read in part:

Resolved by the Senate and House of Representatives of the United States of America in Congress assembled, that in recognition of the achievements of Rear Admiral Hyman George Rickover, United States Navy, in successfully directing the development and construction of the world's first nuclear-powered ships and the first large-scale nuclear power reactor devoted exclusively to production of electricity, the Chairman of the Joint Committee on Atomic Energy, on behalf of the Congress is authorized to present to Admiral Hyman George Rickover, USN, an appropriate gold medal.

On April 15, 1959, Senator Clinton P. Anderson of New Mexico, chairman of the joint committee, read the same words to a distinguished assembly. Present was the full membership of the committee; Rickover's closest and strongest allies in the battle for the nuclear Navy were there. Other top Congressional leaders were present, Senate Majority Leader Lyndon B. Johnson and Minority Leader Everett M. Dirksen among them. The Honorable John A. McCone, chairman of the Atomic Energy Commission, Navy Secretary Gates, and Chief of Naval Operations Admiral Arleigh Burke also stood at attention.

Anderson, speaking into a half-dozen television and radio microphones, said, "In the annals of modern science and technology there have been few efforts more successful than his.

"He has contributed immeasurably to the defense of our nation and concurrently demonstrated the peaceful intentions of the United States in atomic energy. He directed the development and construction of the Shippingport Atomic Power Station—the first full-scale peaceful atomic plant in the United States. Within the Navy, Admiral Rickover made possible a new strategic weapons system of paramount importance in the missile age—the first ballistic missile submarine. His attack submarines promise the control of the seas in event of war."

Majority Leader Lyndon Johnson took the microphone to relate how a year before, Anderson had accosted him in a big rush, saying, "I have a little resolution that won't cost much money but will bring great results to this nation. I want it passed by unanimous consent." Johnson said, "Before I had a chance to call it up, I found that he was going to pass it by unanimous consent because he had practically every member of the Senate as sponsor of it."

He continued, "We meet here to honor a man and to honor an achievement, to honor an uncommon man and an uncommon achievement." Then, pointing out that Congress has often given the armed services more than they wanted: "Nevertheless, when it came to launching this uncommon man on this uncommon venture, we had to renovate a rest room to provide him with an office. We hadn't made a provision for that in our services.

"Admiral, I think we should say to the rest of the world that you are our secret weapon. You are a symbol of the 'can do' man," Johnson said.

In token return, Rickover presented the committee with a bottle of water from the North Pole. Then he told the committee a few facts about the program.

The most important development from a technical standpoint, he said, "is the considerable increase in the life of the nuclear cores, greatly extending the cruising range of our nuclear-powered ships." In addition, there had been operational records set. The *Nautilus*, on her first nuclear core, steamed more than 62,000 miles. "On her present second core," he said, "the *Nautilus* has already steamed more than 80,000 miles and still has energy left in the core. We are now designing nuclear cores that should enable ships to operate for an entire war without refueling."

Rickover continued, "The *Nautilus* last year steamed nonstop from Honolulu to England, a distance of more than 8,000 miles, during which time she traveled 1,830 miles under the polar ice cap. The *Skate* a few days later went under the North Pole from the other direction, east to west, and then made the shortest circuit around the earth that has ever been made. She went around the earth in one hour!"

As the Congressmen expressed amazement, he went on, "She was only one mile from the pole, but this is still the record. I suppose someday an airplane will just spin around the pole and so make it in even shorter time; nevertheless, today the *Skate* holds the record for circumnavigation of the globe."

Rickover also disclosed some more news. A few days previously, he told the group, the *Skate* again steamed under the North Pole. "This time she was under the polar ice for 3,000 miles continuously; she demonstrated that we can operate our submarines at will in the Arctic. This also means that when we have developed submarines that can carry Polaris ballistic missiles, these submarines can remain undetected in the dark polar seas, hidden from an enemy. If an enemy dared to attack the United States, even if he were successful in destroying the United States, he will know that he himself would inevitably be destroyed."

Then the tough-spoken admiral, not given to handing out compliments gratuitously, gave high praise to the men of the nuclear Navy: "Some of the very fine officers who have piloted these ships are in the audience. I am more proud of what these young men have done than I am of what we have done with atomic power. With officers such as these and their highly devoted crews, there is nothing our country cannot do. When people of their caliber are exposed to the challenge and opportunity of our nuclear power program, the results go beyond all expectations. Not only do we get these outstanding operational crews, but individual officers and sailors go on to do an outstanding job in other parts of the Navy as well."

Before presenting the medal, Senator Anderson explained its meaning. "Different countries have different ways of rewarding distinguished and meritorious achievements. In Great Britain a man who was personally responsible for giving his country a position of world leadership in submarine warfare might well be elevated to knighthood; in Belgium such a man might receive the Order of the Crown. France could give him the Legion of Honor.

"But the United States is not a country of heraldry. Our high awards, such as the Congressional Medal of Honor, are usually reserved for valor on the battlefield. For this reason, the Congress of the United States, beginning with the birth of our nation in 1776, has ordered gold medals struck to honor the nation's outstanding citizens. The first gold medal bestowed by Congressional resolution was given to General Washington in 1776," Anderson said.

Only two other Navy admirals had been so honored, Rickover was told. These were the famed polar explorer Richard Byrd and the man who made such a contribution to World War II, Fleet Admiral Ernest J. King. John Paul Jones also received one, but he was a member of the Russian Navy, not the U.S. Navy. Admirals Matthew Perry and George Dewey had received only silver and bronze medals. The medal was conferred on Rickover with a standing ovation.

The tough little admiral, more used to being fought or ignored than so honored, was obviously touched. "There are times when one is too deeply moved to express his feelings. How can I put into words my gratitude, as I stand before you—the busy leaders of our great country who have taken time out from your heavy responsibilities to honor me? It is not enough that I thank you from the bottom of my heart.

"I speak not only for myself but for all the devoted and hardworking members of the Naval reactors group when I pledge that we shall continue our work with renewed enthusiasm and strength. We shall let nothing deter us from building a nuclear Navy in the shortest possible time."

He acknowledged his debt to the Joint Committee on Atomic Energy: "My colleagues and I know that without the committee's active help on countless occasions, and the continuous support of the Congress, we should not now have a single nuclear ship.

"For your never-failing understanding, your friendship, and your kindness in awarding me this medal, I thank you."

11

Exploration

On Saturday, April 11, 1959, another record meeting of the Joint Committee on Atomic Energy was held. Senator Clinton P. Anderson convened the meeting in executive session aboard the U.S.S. nuclear submarine *Skipjack,* more than 400 feet below the surface of the Atlantic Ocean and approximately 135 nautical miles out of New London, Connecticut.

Rickover told the committee about the polar voyages made by the *Nautilus* and the *Skate.* "The real significance of these polar voyages is that another large area of the world—larger than the whole United States—which was heretofore secure from war, has now been exposed by these exploits.

"The entire northern coastline of Russia, formerly protected by the Arctic ice pack, is now exposed. And of course the same applies to Alaska and to Canada," he continued.

The joint committee was intensely interested in hearing about the relative strength of the United States and the Soviet Union.

Senator Anderson told Rickover, "I am happy to participate in this second record-breaking action. The members of the joint committee are very confident that you and your team will continue to lead the world in this area. There is no argument about it. There may be arguments about other programs, but in this one there isn't."

Again, Rickover stressed the advantages of American superiority in the submarine force. "In a large surface-ship task force," he pointed out, "the Navy makes a tremendous investment to get a self-sufficient offensive capability where and when it wants it, with a capability for staying there and doing a job. Now in the nuclear submarine we have such a capability at low cost. The ocean acts as its protecting screen and as its armor.

"As a result, the submarine can be made all weapon, rather than part weapon and part shield. Therefore, we should look at each new improved feature which is added to the submarine as an increase in the effectiveness of this one ship task force rather than concern ourselves unduly over the fact that the submarine may be getting bigger than other submarines or bigger than somebody's idea of an underwater 'pursuit ship.'

"With this concept in mind we lay out the machinery in these ships so that the ship's force can maintain it. We also provide installed spares of all important equipment wherever practicable. This permits the ships to stay at sea for several months and even to stay submerged for two months or more."

The *Skipjack,* Rickover pointed out, was the fastest submarine in the world. Surface ships often couldn't make her maximum speed because of the variable surface conditions at sea or because of heavy weather.

At that very moment, he told the committee members, the *Skipjack* set a new depth record at the highest speed recorded thus far. "This is the first Congressional committee that has ever deliberated so deeply and so fast."

The question of what the Russians might be doing increasingly bothered Rickover. He told another Congressional committee that the Russians had about 500 submarines and the capacity to build about 100 conventionally powered submarines each year.

"But recently they have slowed their rate of building submarines. That might be for one of two reasons. Either they believe they have a sufficient number to carry out the purposes for which they have built these ships, or they are shifting over to a new type," Rickover told the committee.

"I would anticipate that in the not too distant future they will have an operational missile with a range of about 600 to 700 miles. Therefore, with a large number of submarines that can carry missiles fitted with atomic or hydrogen warheads, they have the capacity to operate off our coasts and destroy our cities.

"In my opinion, sir, that is the gravest immediate threat that faces the United States. The best way I know to counter this threat is by means of our own nuclear-powered attack submarines.

"We do not know definitely whether the Russians are working on an atomic-powered submarine. I should imagine they would be."

To Rickover's mind, progress in converting the Navy to an all-nuclear status was not going fast enough. In March, 1959, he told the joint committee: "My sentiments are, as I have often expressed them, that there is great importance in having more nuclear attack submarines to kill off Russian submarines that might attack our coast. The Polaris submarines are a separate function. I am a strong proponent of the Polaris subs, but in my opinion the most important thing for us right now is to build attack submarines to kill off Russian submarines that can launch missiles on our cities."

One of the things he wanted to get going on was a new reactor design, which he described as a natural circulation reactor. "It could result in substantial improvement and simplicity, reliability, and inherent safety of naval pressurized water plants." The reactor itself would be based on the same principle as the previous reactors, but larger. However, by use of heat exchangers, the water could be made to circulate without the use of pumps. Much machinery would be eliminated, including the pumps, piping, and controls for the pumping system, and the generating capacity needed to drive the pumps.

The Navy had given its approval of the project. However, the Atomic Energy Commission was dragging its feet. Although it agreed in principle, it refused to give Rickover funds to begin construction of a land prototype at Arco, Idaho.

Rickover laid his case before the Joint Committee on Atomic Energy. "The only thing I could wait for is until the Russians have one. Then you would be chiding me for not having done it before. I am accused all the time of not being venturesome enough. The General Advisory Committee (to the AEC) says I am not venturesome enough.

"Every time I come up with something I can't get it. I am in a dilemma here. I am too venturesome and I am not venturesome enough," he said with a smile.

Rickover explained why he was so anxious to get started on the project. "I predict it will take two and a half years to build the land-based model. If we delay, it would take three and a half years. That means if I delay, I delay eight submarines which could have a superior plant.

"What I see is eight more obsolete ships which cost forty to fifty million dollars apiece. Not obsolete, but not as good as they could be." The Congressmen shuddered.

Representative Chet Holifield posed a question: "You think the technology has been advanced far enough that you are justified in gambling this amount of money on the model?"

Rickover answered without hesitation. "I don't gamble much. I think you know that if I come against a situation, Mr. Holifield, where I think it is wrong, I would kill it immediately."

They remembered how he had ordered the ship-yard to rip out the sodium-cooled reactor in the

Seawolf submarine, and what he had said then. "It takes courage to do so, to stop things, because people are afraid of blame. Nevertheless a man who heads up a large project has got to be strong and cold-blooded as a surgeon and say, 'This is not good. I must stop it.' We have stopped a number of things, but it is difficult to kill one's brain children. It takes courage," he said somewhat sadly.

Rickover's hopes for a nuclear destroyer fleet also were not progressing as well as some would have liked. Representative Clarence Cannon, powerful chairman of the House Appropriations Committee, looked puzzled as he considered the new budget before him in June, 1959.

"I'm a little surprised to note that the Navy has not included a nuclear destroyer in the fiscal year 1960 shipbuilding program," he said to Rickover.

"We are ready to build more" Rickover admitted. He also noted that the nuclear destroyer being built in the 1959 shipbuilding program would be done before the conventional destroyers which were started in the 1958 program.

While the nuclear version would cost $40,000,000 more than the conventional one, this would include the fuel for the first three or four years. The nuclear destroyer would be able to steam for 100,000 to 150,000 miles continuously at full power. "If a war were to break out today, if our oil supplies were to be cut off, we would not be dependent on scarce oil. So there is a big dividend from having nuclear-powered ships. You can actually store up labor and material during peacetime which does not spoil prior to the war.

"In the last war," he pointed out, "the thing that limited our output was our availability of labor. With nuclear power, you have the opportunity to use that labor in peacetime and to store it. You can put all of the nuclear cores you would use in the entire Navy for a whole war into a couple of warehouses. You would not have to build tankers to carry oil. You would not have to build oil tank farms or make the steel to build them. You would have the nuclear fuel already available."

Rickover expressed his fears about the Soviet threat. "The icebreaker *Lenin* has three nuclear reactors," he told them. "I assume that this ship will be used to try out these reactors, and if they can operate these reactors successfully on the *Lenin,* there is no reason why they cannot operate them successfully in a submarine. So I believe that in a relatively short time the Russians will have nuclear submarines. And since they have the capacity to build one hundred submarines a year, they can outstrip us in a very few years."

To the distressed Congressmen, he said, "We should take advantage of the lead we presently have and exploit it. We are not exploiting it enough. The great danger we face from Russian submarines is an attack on our country, particularly on our coastal cities, by Russian submarines that carry missiles."

Rickover related how, when he was in the submarine service between the two world wars, he saw statements then that the United States was overcoming the German submarine menace. "Looking back, it is plain that we were almost dormant in that effort. We did not make much progress between the two wars, and we nearly lost the last war because of that.

"My opinion is that, relatively, we are no better off today than we were before 1941," he said. This was shocking news indeed to the committee. He explained, "That is, we are in no better position to defeat today's Russian submarine menace than we were to defeat the German submarine threat in 1941. If fortune favors us and we have the privilege of looking back from the vantage point of ten to fifteen years from now, we probably will find that relative to today's requirements we are doing no better than we did between the two world wars—that we have not learned the lesson. I believe the main function of the Navy should be antisubmarine warfare—to defeat the Russian submarine menace."

Warnings about the Soviet threat seemed out of place during that hot summer. The United States was enjoying a time of particularly good relations with Russia, marked by the visit to America of Frol R. Kozlov, first deputy premier of the Soviet Union.

Followed by a handful of newsmen, Rickover escorted the Russian official through the Shippingport nuclear power plant. There he explained in general terms the functions of the plant and answered his eager questions.

During the tour, Rickover told Kozlov that he was a Naval officer whose interest was in building atomic submarines. Kozlov retorted, "It would be better to build atomic surface vessels rather than atomic submarines because atomic submarines are for the purpose of destruction."

According to newsmen present, Rickover's only

answer was, "Sure, all Soviet naval vessels have doves of peace on their masts."

Two weeks later the Soviets played hosts to the Vice President of the United States, Richard Nixon, and his official party. Representing the Navy in this group was Admiral Rickover.

The admiral, of course, tried his best to get a look at Soviet atomic developments, going first to the shipyard where the atomic icebreaker *Lenin* was docked. Reporters waited for two hours while he poked about the vessel, studying its equipment and crawling into its nooks and crannies so as not to miss anything.

Upon the return of the group from Russia, the official announcement came from the Defense Department that the Soviets were building nuclear-powered submarines and missiles equivalent to the Polaris missile as well as intercontinental missiles.

Rickover was immediately called by Congress to give a report on what he saw. As he introduced him, Representative Cannon said, "We are honored by having with us today one of the most distinguished men of the nation, the Father of Nuclear Propulsion. The nation probably would not be safe except for the contributions of Admiral Rickover in the adaptation of nuclear power to submarines and the utilization of atomic energy in both military and civilian enterprises."

But Rickover talked not only about military might; something else had struck him strongly during his visit to Russia.

"My visit to Russia and Poland confirmed my belief that the real race we are in with Communism is to see whose educational system best prepares youth for the world of modern science and technology.

"I had the opportunity to talk to the minister of education in both Russia and Poland, and with other educational officials. I came away from this visit feeling that the Russian educational system, in part, has been designed more efficiently to serve their national and ideological objectives than our school system serves the objectives of our democratic capitalism.

"The number of Russians graduated from their ten-year schools is about the same as the number of American graduates from our high schools, but the Russians are at least two years ahead of the American high school graduates in sound, basic education.

"By that I mean mathematics, the sciences, mastery of the mother tongue, knowledge of their own classic literature and that of major foreign nations, foreign languages, and history—although their history is colored by Marxist doctrine."

Education became a crusade for the admiral, who brought to this new interest the same kind of single-minded zeal he gave to the nuclear naval program. He made a careful study of different educational systems, noting the good and bad points of each and the results of these on the students. He saw many things which disturbed him in the American school system.

He began lecturing meetings of citizens' groups and in fact became such an expert that he was invited to address educators themselves. As usual, his views produced some controversial reactions; school principals hardly liked hearing that they were doing things badly. He began to write long articles in national magazines in the hope of reaching the widest possible audience.

Once asked for his advice to young people, he replied: "If God gave me the opportunity to know, at their age, what I now know, I certainly would work a lot harder. I would try to become a scientist or engineer, but I would not forget the humanities. I would also study much harder."

He even suggested to Congress some ideas he thought might help to remedy the shortcomings of American education. First, he said, eliminate four years in the educational cycle by eliminating all extraneous matter. It would be a great boon, he observed, if the school process were reduced by three or four years.

The Russians, he pointed out, were graduating about 120,000 engineers a year, while the United States graduated only about 40,000. In a few years the Soviets would step that figure up to 145,000. In all of Russia, there were more than a million engineers, while the United States had only a little more than half that number of practicing engineers.

"Even if the Cold War were to end tomorrow, we would still be competing industrially with the Soviets," he pointed out. Forty years before, the Soviet Union stood tenth in industrial production in the world. But in those forty years she rose to second place. "She rose from a time when half of her people were illiterate until today her illiteracy rate is no worse, probably better, than ours," he said.

He also issued another strong warning. The great dogmatist of Communism, Nikolai Lenin, had foreseen the world struggle which would occur between

181

Western civilization and totalitarian Communism. His advice to the Communists was that the soundest strategy in war would be to postpone operations until the moral disintegration of the enemy made him so weak and soft that the mortal blow would be possible and, in fact, very easy.

"Many thoughtful observers of the American scene believe that the seed of moral disintegration is present in our system of public education, and that unless the recent trend of that system toward mediocrity can be checked, we will be seriously, perhaps mortally, incapacitated in our individual and national ability to defend the values of the Western world against strong ideological competition," Rickover warned.

"The American people must be alerted to the deficiencies of our school system and adopt ways in which we can reform our schools. Unless we reform our schools in the interests of producing liberally educated citizens in the aggregate, we will not be able to cope with the most serious challenge ever to face our country," he told Congress.

Rickover's proposal was not to copy the education systems of any other country but to take lessons from certain aspects of some foreign educational systems. Most particularly, he emphasized the need for achieving in the United States the same serious attitude toward education that was expressed in other countries.

There is no doubt that his efforts, and those of other top scientists and engineers, had a tremendous impact on educators. The easy social courses which had crept into American school curricula were seriously examined, and many were thrown out. In their place, new techniques in teaching mathematics, new extensive courses in sciences, and discipline in the basics of reading, spelling, and languages was emphasized. The country went through an intellectual rebirth, however haltingly, as it entered the new technological age of the 1960's.

Admiral Rickover spared no criticism of his own alma mater, the Naval Academy. "I interviewed some ninety of the top-ranking first classmen in my office in Washington to determine whether they were qualified for entry into the nuclear training program," he said in 1961.

"The major thing that comes out of the interviews is that the midshipmen are quite immature in their attitude. . . . Instead of using these very impressionable years from sixteen to twenty-two to train them for a serious adult occupation, the Naval Academy authorities treat them as adolescents, and they react accordingly."

By contrast, Rickover said, in civilian universities the men were thrown on their own. But at the Naval Academy, "almost everything is done for them. They are subject to petty rules, many of which had their origin back in English boarding schools but no longer have any meaning in this day and age.

"The term 'brigade of midshipmen' is no misnomer," he said. "They are a regimented group. They are being trained for a Navy which no longer exists— by officers, many of whom do not know the real needs of today's Navy and who are not aware that they don't know." This was practically blasphemy to the school-book Navy officers who placed great store in the tradition and trappings of their Annapolis days.

Rickover also noted that he had interviewed Naval Reserve Officers Training Corps midshipmen from civilian colleges. By comparison, he said, the young men from the civilian colleges were more adult in their attitudes, and they were generally better qualified academically.

"A more serious defect even than the deficiency in scholarship is the attitude the midshipmen acquire at the Naval Academy," he said. "Once he graduates he will, in nine cases out of ten, stop thinking and studying."

One of the problems, Rickover grumbled, was the kind of thing which happened to one young midshipman whose class standing had been near the top up to his senior year, but then suddenly dropped. When the admiral asked him why, the youth replied that during the first week of the year, he had been chosen with a group of midshipmen to be escorts to the Miss America contest candidates. During the second year, it turned out, he was sent to Mexico with another group of midshipmen representing the Naval Academy. On top of that, he was active in some five extracurricular activities, much stressed at the academy.

"Here was a fine young man with a good mind frittering away his time with trivia, taking no elective courses, and performing academically way below his capabilities," he said. Rickover also criticized the heavy emphasis on sports such as football, which also contributed to bring the boy's grades down. To the suggestion that football developed initiative and leadership, he sniffed. "I have never understood how these qualities are developed in carrying out plays which are selected by the coach, and which require precise movements laid out in advance by him."

The iconoclastic admiral also scorned the psychiatrists' reports which purported to define which kind of boy succeeded at the service academies. At West Point, he pointed out, a psychiatric board concluded that boys who were close to their fathers and "identified" with the male role got along best, while those whose mothers were domineering and overprotective and who didn't get along with their fathers couldn't make the grade.

"On the basis of this study I doubt Alexander the Great, Hannibal, Julius Caesar, Napoleon, George Washington, John Paul Jones, Stephen Decatur, U. S. Grant, or David Farragut could have made the grade at West Point," he said, laughing.

"I view with horror the day the Navy is induced to place psychiatrists aboard our nuclear submarines. We are doing very well without them because the men don't know they have problems. But once a psychiatrist is assigned, they will learn that they have lots of problems!"

And, as Rickover rightly pointed out, no psychiatrists were on the nuclear subs and the men weren't having any visible problems. In fact, on May 10, 1960, another epic record was chalked up by the nuclear submarine force. The *Triton* surfaced on that day after traveling underseas all the way around the world, closely paralleling the route of Magellan in 1519 through 1522.

The trip had begun on February 16. The purpose

was to determine whether a nuclear-powered vessel could travel submerged halfway around the world, fire her missiles at the enemy, and return again to the United States without once showing herself on the surface.

Eighty-four days and 41,500 miles later the answer was most conclusively given: Yes.

And on a hot August day in 1960, the Polaris missile was proving out the other half of the question. In the early humid dawn, the U.S.S. *George Washington,* the first nuclear ballistic missile submarine, made her way out to a point about 30 miles from Cape Canaveral.

The submarine was jam-packed with a double crew and a host of top Navy officials and industrial representatives, some along for the honor of the occasion, the others to give last-minute technical advice if needed. For almost two days the crew had been plagued with communications blackouts, radar problems, and weather squalls, meaning postponement of the crucial test.

But after a six-hour countdown, the moment approached for the first submerged launch of the Polaris missile. Hovering about 40 feet below the surface, the submarine was made ready for the launch. "Get hot and stay hot," Commander James Osborn barked to his crew.

In the center of the submarine, in the area nicknamed Sherwood Forest, stood sixteen Polaris missiles, erect and ready to go. Each stood in its own green-painted, plastic potted tube.

About one minute before the launch, a warning smoke bomb was set off. Commander Osborn pushed a green go-button, and the signal traveled to missile number nine. Compressed air was injected into the base of the tube, pushing the missile upward with a swoosh through a watertight hatch which opened on command.

The big question in everyone's mind was whether the highly sophisticated launching system could actually compensate for the rocking of the ship and send the missile in the right direction.

But each position was calculated by three ship's inertial navigation systems and a digital computer which checked each against the others. The information fed by SINS, the ship's star tracker, whereby speed and ocean current data were fed into the fire control system, made the final calculation on how to direct the missile.

On the surface, the needle nose of the Polaris first broke through the glassy calm, followed by its short, stubby body, which churned up a tremendous white wake.

The officers gasped as they saw that the missile was 15 degrees off the vertical, which meant that she would nose into the water far short of the target. But then the jetavators took over and straightened the column upright once more. When she was six feet above the surface, the first stage ignited, burning one minute to produce 65,000 pounds of thrust.

Over the ship's loudspeaker the second-stage ignition was announced, and the crew knew the Polaris was on her way. The first missile reached an altitude of about 400 miles and flew an impressive 1,000 miles down the Atlantic Missile Range. Three hours later, Osborn ordered another one fired. This one moved flawlessly upward out of the water and joined the first in the bull's-eye of the target zone.

Osborne radioed this message to Navy operations and to Washington:

This new sea star of peace hoisted a trail of missile smoke from salt water to space as a signal of a bright new addition to sea power, a new strategic use of the world's oceans, a new free-world ballistic peace force. We can all be glad that this is another American worldwide first.

12

The Fight Continues

Nuclear submarines were only the beginning, however. If the battle against obstinate tradition was finally won as far as undersea vessels were concerned, it was just beginning for the surface Navy. And no one would need more than one guess as to who was in the thick of it.

The crusade again was launched: the trips back and forth to the Navy's top offices with documents designed to show the advantages of nuclear propulsion, the late hours, the endless memorandums, the mountains of paperwork which form the ammunition piles of the bureaucratic war.

Again, Congress became Rickover's strongest ally. The usual chain of events went something like this: The nuclear propulsion proponents would campaign for a nuclear surface ship, perhaps a destroyer or an aircraft carrier. The Navy, or perhaps the Secretary of

Defense, would refuse. Meanwhile, the Rickover group would manage to get work on the reactor portion going through the Atomic Energy Commission.

Congress would hear about it and call the Defense Department on the carpet to ask why it wasn't requesting funds for nuclear vessels. The Defense Department would say they were too expensive or make some other excuse. But Congress, with its great admiration for the outspoken admiral who headed the nuclear program, would add money to the defense budget and demand that work begin immediately.

Sometimes the Defense Department listened, and sometimes it dragged its feet for years. As early as 1961, the House Armed Services Committee made its feelings known in no uncertain terms, ordering that the plans for the frigate the U.S.S. *Truxton,* for which the Navy was requesting funds, be changed from conventional to nuclear propulsion.

"We want to increase the number of surface naval vessels which will possess the invaluable ability to cruise with almost unlimited endurance," the committee report said in effect.

At about this time, the United States' first nuclear aircraft carrier, the *Enterprise,* was putting out to sea. Rickover again played host to the Joint Committee on Atomic Energy on the *Enterprise,* showing the awed Congressmen about the streamlined, powerful vessel.

But as they moved down the deck, Rickover turned to them in some exasperation. "The situation now facing us is just like that with nuclear submarines in 1955 when the joint committee first went to sea in the *Nautilus*," he told them.

"The objection to building nuclear subs at that time was that Congress was appropriating about $40,000,000 a year for one conventional sub," he pointed out. "The people in Naval Operations were afraid that if we changed from conventional to nuclear subs, they might get two every three years instead of one every year, so they were opposed to the nuclear submarines."

Emphatically he made his point. "Exactly the same situation prevails today with regard to the surface Navy. You get hurled at you figures showing nuclear power for a surface ship is 1.3 to 1.5 times as expensive as a conventional ship; that is, a nuclear ship costs 30 to 50 percent more than a conventional one."

He had his ammunition ready for the argument. "So I thought it interesting to quote a few cost figures on other important weapons. In comparison to World War Two costs with costs today for various items of military equipment, an Army rifle went up from $31 to $100. Conventional destroyers went from $9,000,000 to $35,000,000—four times. Highways went from $150,000 a mile to $775,000 a mile; a strategic bomber from $300,000 to $9,300,000, thirty-one times.

"You never hear a word from the Navy that because of the higher cost of the airplanes on this ship we shouldn't have them; but you do hear that nuclear power is 1.3 times as expensive, and that is why we can't have more nuclear-powered surface ships," he concluded.

It seems, the admiral continued, that if modern weapons are to be evaluated only on a cost basis, Congress could argue that there is twenty times as much justification for not having the most modern propulsion plant. "As a matter of fact, since the cost of having babies has gone up 1.7 times, on this same basis it would be quite the thing that we cut down on the number of children!" he exclaimed.

But the big argument, not accounted for by the cost figures, was the military advantages of the nuclear carrier, unequaled by the conventionally powered counterpart. Rickover's own belief, he said, was that three nuclear vessels would be worth four conventional ones. The nuclear aircraft carrier could carry more fuel for the aircraft on its deck, so that the force would have much more effectiveness and more hours in operation. It also would be less vulnerable to submarine attack because of its high speed and the fact that it would not have to slow down to the speed of an oiler to refuel.

"It's the same as in 1955," Rickover sighed. "The Navy had to have the *Nautilus* before they could envision it. The Naval officers had to go on board and ride it at sea before they could make up their minds it was worthwhile. We have the same thing again with the surface ships. Somebody has to force through the first one and then after the officers ride it, they say, 'My, this is a fine ship. Why haven't we had more of them?' "

Rickover made a plea to the committee. "This

meeting tonight is historic because I think the committee can be just as influential for our surface Navy as it was for our submarine Navy. You are the ones who forced the nuclear submarine Navy. I think without your forcing we will not have a nuclear surface Navy."

Once again he had spoken bluntly, far more so than any other military officer in recent history. His words were veritable mutiny, going against his superiors so openly and candidly. The battle was out in the open. But the Navy and the Defense Department now knew better than to try to quash the gadfly by passing over him or insulting him. Congress was squarely on his side, and if the Defense Department wanted to get money for anything it wanted at all, it could not afford to defy the wishes of Congress too often.

The giant carrier *Enterprise,* running smoothly and powerfully, was an excellent salesman for the nuclear surface force itself. When in November, 1962, the world was shaken with another explosion in the Cold War, when Communist Russia decided to try to put long-range missiles on Cuba and aim them at the United States, President John F. Kennedy decided to call the Soviet bluff. The *Enterprise* was sent to lead a task force together with the conventional carrier the *Independence* to blockade the island from the reach of missile-bearing Soviet ships.

The commander of this task force was Rear Admiral J. T. Hayward. In a letter to the Secretary of the Navy, Fred Korth, he wrote: "My experience in the *Enterprise* to date has convinced me more than ever that the military advantages of nuclear propulsion in surface combatant ships more than outweigh their extra cost."

Admiral Hayward reminded Korth that Hayward had been one of the few who had been in favor of building another nuclear carrier. "I wish that those who dismiss the admitted advantages of nuclear power as not being worth the extra cost could have shared our experiences during the past two months on the Cuban blockade. It is now even more obvious to me that the CVA-67 should have nuclear propulsion."

Hayward went on to describe how more than 10,000 landings had been made on the deck of the *Enterprise* during her first year of operation, a record unsurpassed by any other carrier in the fleet. Her planes were easier and cheaper to maintain and were combat-ready more of the time because they were not corroded by the harsh stack gases put out by conventional power plants. Her propulsion plant was rugged and she could travel at sustained high speeds and maneuver easily, making air operations far easier. And without the huge boiler uptakes on deck, communication and radar systems were unobstructed. "In Washington these often cited advantages of nuclear propulsion seem to get lost in a shuffle of paper—in Cuba they were real," Hayward emphasized.

"I think the Cuban crisis made all of us do a lot more thinking about how we will fare in war. On blockade duty our conventional escorts were usually refueled every other day. Protecting that oil supply train under air and submarine attack would have been tough enough right here in our own backyard—in an advanced area the problem will be magnified many-fold," Hayward pointed out.

To maintain fleets at sea against the hostile forces that are sure to oppose us will require every technical advantage we can possibly muster, the admiral wrote. "Frankly, Mr. Korth, I am deeply disturbed that we are not exploiting to the fullest the technical advantages we hold in nuclear propulsion that has been gained through such great effort. I do not believe you can weigh victory or defeat on a scale of dollars and cents—yet the margin between victory and defeat in future naval engagements may well depend on the availability of nuclear-powered ships to the fleet commander of the future."

Strong words, indeed. But in spite of the widespread support in the Navy, there was an almost insurmountable hurdle in the fact that, without question, nuclear power was expensive and more so than conventional power plants.

It was the time of the new Defense Secretary, Robert Strange McNamara, who revolutionized the Defense Department with new efficiency and eliminated wasteful duplication and interservice rivalries by harnessing the military services under his own, single control. Accompanied by bespectacled "Whiz Kids" who brought intellectual and management talents never before seen in the Pentagon, McNamara put great emphasis on economy and "cost effectiveness."

Cost effectiveness meant that each weapons system was measured against any other which might fulfill the same role, and the price tags compared. The price tag for conventional carriers was unquestionably less than that for nuclear.

So, on the heels of the *Enterprise*'s great performance and the fine record of the other two existing nuclear surface vessels, the guided missile cruiser the *Long Beach* and the destroyer the *Bainbridge,* Secretary McNamara decided to build a conventional carrier.

When McNamara dropped his bombshell on the Navy, he wrote Navy Secretary Fred Korth a memorandum: "I understand that nuclear-powered task forces have very desirable characteristics. However, the real choice we face is not between a given number of conventional ships for one sum of money and the same number of nuclear ships for a larger sum. The choice is between a given number of conventional ships and a smaller number of nuclear ships at the same total cost."

In other words, the Defense Department was insisting on one price. And it could get more conventional ships for that price than nuclear, no matter how superior they might be. Asked about the decision in Congress, Secretary McNamara said, "This is what we do all the time. We don't buy the best there is in terms of technology in any one of our weapons systems."

To the irritation of many of the Congressmen he continued: "We would be foolish if we bought the best in technology in terms of the most advanced in terms of speed and range and firepower, when we don't need it. The fact is, I could give you twenty illustrations of where we have not bought the best in terms of modern technology because we don't need it. We should only buy what we need and what we need is usable effective combat power. That is the only standard we are applying."

What was "really needed" by the country would continue to be a matter of great controversy among Secretary McNamara, the Navy, and the Congress for many years to come.

Some of the Navy's top brass complained bitterly about Secretary McNamara's decision. Vice-Admiral Hayward, now commander of the Pacific antisubmarine warfare forces, wrote to Senator John Pastore of the Joint Committee on Atomic Energy: "It is indeed unfortunate that we have not been able to convince the Secretary of Defense of the meaning of true mobility at sea."

"We have no argument with civilian control, but as the saying goes about Hannibal, 'If we are told to cross the Alps, I would like at least to be able to pick the elephants!' "said Hayward.

The irony of the whole thing was that the CVA-67, over which the controversy raged, would later be renamed the carrier *John F. Kennedy* in honor of the assassinated President.

About this time, Admiral Hyman Rickover's fate was once again on the decision table. In January, 1964, he would be sixty-four, the Navy's mandatory age for retirement. But almost a year before, his admirers started making sure he would not be allowed to disappear from the scene, no matter how much the top level of the Defense Department might have wanted him to.

Members of Congress began quietly approaching

him. Senator Bourke Hickenlooper, a member of the Joint Committee on Atomic Energy, was typical.

"I'm concerned about two things, Admiral. I'm concerned about your personal future in this program. It is important that you stay on. I am also concerned about the future of your group and the future of the program if you should leave it. I would not want anything to destroy what you have built up."

Representative Melvin Price was another. "I do not think Congress is going to stand idly by and watch you put on the shelf. Congress has expressed itself before on this matter, and if further action is required, we are not reluctant to act."

And they weren't reluctant to act. But this time the Navy at last supported its in-house critic. After a few meetings at the White House and the Pentagon, some important announcements were made.

First, at the White House, President Johnson nominated Admiral Rickover for retirement with the permanent rank of vice-admiral. His rank at the time was rear admiral.

Still more important, the Navy Secretary announced that Admiral Rickover would be called to active duty after he went through the motions of retiring on February 1. The Navy indicated that as long as he wanted to serve, he would be welcomed with the same authority he then had, and in the same position.

As usual, despite any questions which might have been raised around him concerning his future, Rickover continued on the course he had set out for himself, unperturbed by personal considerations.

It was decided in the spring of 1964 that a major demonstration would have to be made of the advantages of nuclear power to the surface fleet.

The whole nuclear fleet—consisting of three vessels, the carrier U.S.S. *Enterprise,* the cruiser U.S.S. *Long Beach,* and the frigate U.S.S. *Bainbridge*— would have to do something that no other ships could do. That way, it was hoped, the lesson of nuclear power could be brought home to the civilians in the Pentagon who opposed it because it cost too much.

On July 31, 1964, the three vessels began a world cruise in the Mediterranean Sea, where they had been brought to form the world's first nuclear task force. Task Force 1, as it was dubbed, took a 30,500-mile voyage in which it circled Africa and touched briefly in Asia during a port visit to Karachi, Pakistan. The three ships parted company in Australia, where each made a visit to a different Australian port, then rejoined one another for the long trek across the Pacific Ocean around Cape Horn to Norfolk, Virginia.

The entire cruise was traveled at speeds higher than 20 knots and without one stop for repairs, refueling, or restocking of supplies of any kind. Because of the endless power generated by their nuclear reactors, no such stops were necessary. The airplanes assigned to the *Enterprise* carried out daily flight operations from her deck. But she remained completely independent, free of any need of support from shore. As one Navy hand put it, it was a freedom unknown since sailing ship days.

The commander of Nuclear Task Force 1 said later that if any conventional task force commander had received the orders he had for the operation, which

199

was called Operation Sea Orbit, the man would have thought the officers in Navy headquarters were crazy. The orders had read: "Take an aircraft carrier, a cruiser and a frigate to Norfolk from the Mediterranean—the long way. Do it fast and don't expect to get any help at all along the way." Although it would have been impossible with conventional power, he had been able to proceed without question.

Later he wrote, "Operation Sea Orbit was an experience that comes to few men. The true mobility of nuclear-powered ships and their now demonstrated independence from conventional replenishment requirements provide a commander with an advantage hitherto unknown in naval warfare. Their ability to perform day after day at high speeds enables them to move rapidly to nearly any part of the world and at the same time provides defense against air or submarine attack."

The commander-in-chief of the Pacific fleet, Admiral Thomas H. Moorer, added his congratulations: "I see the time when nuclear power will be the predominate means of propelling the fleet. The advantages are so overwhelming that we must take no other course. This change is as inevitable as were the changes from canvas to coal and from coal to oil."

Moorer called Operation Sea Orbit only the beginning of the Navy which would someday be. "The task is far from finished. We must do all we possibly can to ensure that our dedicated Navy men, who are called upon to face the enemy and must daily duel with the dangers of the sea, are provided with the enormous advantages of nuclear propulsion."

Operation Sea Orbit made a large splash indeed. National magazines carried photographic accounts of the unprecedented feat, which proved that the arm of the United States could reach into any corner of the world without help or dependence upon any other country, as long as she had her nuclear fleet. Congressman Craig Hosmer heralded the event as evidence that the U.S. Navy was undergoing another revolutionary change in warship propulsion. The changes from sail to coal, and then from coal to oil, were each resisted bitterly, he recalled. The third revolution, which would move the Navy from oil to the atom, was just as difficult.

"Today the United States is clearly preeminent in the field of nuclear propulsion. But the job is only half done. Despite an encouraging beginning, we still face an uphill fight to complete the conversion of the surface fleet to nuclear power," Hosmer said.

And in spite of the widespread acclamation of Sea Orbit, Hosmer's forecast of the fight ahead proved to be prophetic.

The campaign waged on. Congress, Admiral Moorer, and the indefatigable Rickover collected letters, documents, charts, anything which would help convince the Secretary of Defense of the necessity for a nuclear Navy.

For a time it seemed as though the battle was being won. On November 13, 1964, Navy Secretary Paul H. Nitze wrote to the Secretary of Defense, proposing that a nuclear-powered frigate be included in the fiscal year 1966 budget program. Since the frigate *Truxton*—nuclear by virtue only of Congress' action—had been launched in October, this would have completed the first full all-nuclear task group.

Nitze's arguments were impressive. The addition of another nuclear escort for the carrier *Enterprise* would mean that the ships could hold their antiair-warfare or antisubmarine-warfare stations without lowering their readiness for periodic refueling. The *Enterprise*'s fuel tanks, some of which had to be used to carry fuel for her conventional escort ships, could be turned over completely to aircraft fuel, meaning much more effectiveness for the strike force.

The task force would have a quicker response, for it could travel faster and choose better routes because it did not have to look for ports for refueling. It could trail an enemy submarine or surface ship for long distances with no need to stop.

At the official launching of the *Truxton*, the vice-chairman of the Joint Committee on Atomic Energy reminded the world that it was the Congress that had arranged to buy the nuclear power plants for the first two nuclear submarines—the *Nautilus* and the *Seawolf*—with Atomic Energy Commission funds. This was because the then Captain Hyman George Rickover couldn't get the necessary support from the Department of Defense for his project.

"Let us beware that history does not repeat itself," the chairman said. "The military advantages of nuclear propulsion for naval surface ships have been acknowledged by all. We must be alert to assure that our future capital naval surface ships incorporate the proven advantages of nuclear propulsion."

But history, as the saying goes, did repeat itself.

Although some reactor work was permitted, the Defense Department decided not to build any nuclear surface vessels. Cost effectiveness was king. Secretary McNamara decided that nuclear vessels had a lower priority than developments in other services and turned down the Navy's request for a nuclear frigate to round out the task force.

In fact, when Congress irately questioned McNamara as to his future intentions, it looked very much as though there were no plans to build any more surface ships at all except for a carrier, until 1970.

Congress exploded with anger, feeling that national defense was being jeopardized. Admiral Rickover was hastily summoned for his views, and as always, he was not reluctant to express them.

Rickover reminded Congress that Sir Winston Churchill had to pull a reluctant Royal Navy from the coal age to oil. That navy went on to world leadership as a result of his stubborn leadership, but he had had a tough fight convincing the Admiralty that it should pay the extra price. Churchill himself described the incident in these words:

> Shocked at the expense the Admiralty had reverted for two years to 27-knot coal-burning flotillas. I was too late to stop the last bevy of these inferior vessels, but I gave directions to design the new flotilla to realize 35-knot speed without giving up anything in gunpower, torpedoes, or seaworthiness. I proposed to the board that if money ran short, we should take 16 of these

rather than 20 of the others. Building slow destroyers! One might as well breed slow race horses!

Rickover had his own thoughts about cost effectiveness as well. "The cost-effectiveness people have created the illusion that they are capable of relating cost to military effectiveness by scientific analysis. In actual fact, they are just as reluctant to change preconceived opinions as they accuse the military of being.

"Many people are mesmerized into believing that a study which is based on computer calculations must be correct since it uses the most modern mathematical techniques. They are led to believe that the results are equivalent to scientific proof. This, of course, is just not so."

He pointed out again and again that the numerical studies, which awed so many people and disarmed many opponents of the Defense Department's decisions, were only as good as the assumptions on which they were based. Whether done by computer or by a scientist with a pencil and scrap of paper, the numbers were only as good as the theories on which they were formed.

One thing left out of the computer, Rickover pointed out, was the increased military effectiveness available through nuclear propulsion.

"Now if the Navy could be assured that they would not be asked to perform missions where it would be difficult to get oil to our ships there would be less need for nuclear propulsion," Rickover admitted. But such ideal situations could hardly be depended upon. Military history was full of examples of major defeats brought about by the inability of military forces to get fuel to their combat forces.

Some of the studies also assumed that the forces would not need sustained high-speed endurance to win the war. As Rickover pointed out, when the war comes, the United States will have to fight with what she has, no matter if her assumptions were wrong. Wasn't it better to have the best available to meet any threat?

"On a cost-effective basis the colonists would not have revolted against King George the Third, nor would John Paul Jones have engaged the *Serapis* with the *Bonhomme Richard,* an inferior ship. The Greeks at Thermophylae and at Salamis would not have stood up to the Persians had they cost-effectiveness people to advise them, or had these cost-effectiveness people been in charge. Computer logic would have advised the British to make terms with Hitler in 1940, a course that would have been disastrous to all English-speaking peoples," he pointed out.

One of the most damning bits of evidence, however, was the proof Rickover brought in that the cost-effectiveness studies did not take into account human lives. Rickover pointed to previous testimony by the Chief of Naval Operations, who had admitted that he would expect less loss of life with an all-nuclear group because of its reduced vulnerability and lesser dependence upon resupply operations.

But when he was asked what cost was assigned to these lives, the CNO answered rather reluctantly, "Cost or value associated with American lives is not included in such studies conducted by the Navy. This does not mean that zero cost and zero value are assigned to American lives in the studies. It is simply a recognition of the fact that in order to keep the cost-effectiveness analysis within manageable limits, the cost factors assigned the various elements under study must be both supportable and of finite proportions; that attempting to assign an intrinsic value to a human life would introduce such a questionable and indeed controversial factor into the problem that the objectives of the studies would not be attainable."

In other words, since no one could put limits on what a human life was worth, it was left out of the studies completely!

The battle raged on and on. Admiral Rickover said resignedly that he believed that cost effectiveness eventually would pass, just like all the other "isms" which the United States had embraced with religious fervor from time to time.

But it was a grinding, wearying argument that was carried forth in the Pentagon, spilling over into the halls of the White House and offices of Congress. Congress put money in the Defense bill each year so that the Navy could build the more expensive nuclear vessels instead of the conventional ones chosen in economy's name. But still the Defense Department would refuse to build them.

Meanwhile, the Vietnam War went on. The nuclear carrier *Enterprise* and her escort ship *Bainbridge* performed outstanding combat service off Vietnam, but still the Defense Department refused to build more nuclear ships.

On May 27 the new aircraft carrier was launched. Instead of great praise as CVA-67 came off the ways, the traditional contingent of Congressmen only looked glum.

Back in Washington in the House of Representatives, Congressman Chet Holifield took the floor to tell about it: "Last Saturday we launched our latest aircraft carrier, the *John F. Kennedy*. Our freedom depends on the brave men who will man such ships, but I wonder if we are doing, as a nation, what we should to provide these brave men with the best to do this job.

"*Kennedy*, the aircraft carrier, was obsolete when it was launched," he said. "It is a second-best carrier. It could have been a first-class aircraft carrier if the Secretary of Defense, the Secretary of the Navy, and the Congress had been in agreement and had listened to the advice of the most knowledgeable men in the Navy on the importance of nuclear propulsion.

"What a tragedy that a ship which will have the responsibility of serving, as President Johnson said, 'in the year 2000 and beyond,' has to be shackled with the obsolescence of the oil-propulsion methods of another century, the early decades of the twentieth century.

"What a tragedy that the name of one of our most brilliant and forward-looking Presidents could not have been borne by a modern nuclear propulsion aircraft greater in capability even than the *Enterprise*," Holifield exclaimed in anger.

And the battle continued.

13

The Future

In the more than twenty years which had passed
since the Naval study group at Oak Ridge first
watched the germination of the nuclear Navy seed,
the technology had come both an astoundingly long
way and, at the same time, a painfully short distance.

By the standards of the development of mankind,
the advent of nuclear power was truly incredible. The
atom had been split, its energy had been harnessed,
and the very secret of energy had been unlocked and
made to work for man. Submarines cruised beneath
the ocean for months without seeing the surface,
carrying their deadly weapons as a deterrent against
any nation who would threaten the peace of the
United States.

With the development of the Shippingport plant
under the direction of Admiral Rickover, the country
had gradually embraced the idea of generating elec-

tricity from nuclear energy. By the end of 1962, private industry and the electric utilities, working with the Atomic Energy Commission, had put into operation several smaller light-water reactors around the country to demonstrate how reliable nuclear power could be.

Although they were finally accepted without fear by the citizenry, they did not at first prove to be economically competitive with conventional generating methods. But by the end of 1963, the Jersey Central Power and Light Company contracted for a 515,000-kilowatt nuclear plant at Oyster Creek, New Jersey, which was for the first time competitive with a plant that burned fossil fuel, or coal.

The key, it appeared, was the size of the operation. If large enough, it became economically feasible for the utility company to choose nuclear power instead of coal. The idea caught on rapidly, as is the way in private enterprise, where the word spreads quickly when a cheaper way to do things is discovered. In 1965, ten new nuclear plants were ordered. In 1966, almost thirty more. And each year the number grew.

One of the great advantages of nuclear power is that it is a clean source of power. With the country becoming more and more conscious of its growing air pollution problem, it became clear that in some high-density areas such as California, coal-burning plants would have to be shut down because of the smog and health problem. These were the areas in which power was most important because of the tremendous amount of industrial activity going on. Yet the very act of furnishing the industry with power was contributing to the terrible air pollution problem.

Nuclear energy, however, is a clean source of energy, and nuclear plants do not create combustion products. In fact, Dr. Glen T. Seaborg, chairman of the Atomic Energy Commission, had a vision of a highly automated, nuclear-powered industrial complex that would desalt seawater, process natural resources, recycle old materials, and turn out new products while also supplying electricity to distant cities and transportation systems, all without producing one whiff of smoke or smog.

These complexes, he foresaw, might be partly underground, and would someday allow the country to live in a junkless, unpolluted world where the cities and countryside would be relatively independent of its heavy industry.

Nuclear desalting plants with the dual purpose of producing electricity were planned, with one for the Los Angeles area. Its daily output was to be 1,800,000 kilowatts of electricity and 150,000,000 gallons of desalted seawater per day.

No longer fearsome or even very unusual, nuclear power had come a long way from Shippingport. Nuclear plants were accepted even by the naturalists and horticulturists, who cooperated with the scientists and engineers to incorporate the plants into parks and forests. There they quietly hummed along at the forefront of technology while nature lay almost unspoiled around.

The idea of using nuclear explosions to excavate underground cavities was being looked at in Project

Plowshare. Together with industrial corporations who saw future in the idea, plans were made and carried out by the Atomic Energy Commission to set up controlled blasts to liberate natural gas locked up in the hard shale beneath the ground. Scientists foresaw the day when companies could get into the nuclear rock-crushing business. Oil also would be available through these explosions, they said.

Such blasts could be used to create vast underground storage cavities for natural gas imported into one state from another. Giant catch basins to retain rainfall, 98 percent of which is usually lost to evaporation, also were envisioned.

The world of medicine had been greatly changed by the development of nuclear technology. In hospitals, thirty isotopes of various elements were being used as labels which would help doctors trace the functioning of the vital organs and fluid systems of the interior of the body.

They provided a window to what was going on within without the necessity of laying bare those delicate areas through dangerous, painful, and perhaps needless surgery. Radioisotopes also were being used by industry for testing delicate equipment and tracing the movement of fluids through closed systems.

In agriculture, radiation was used experimentally to preserve food. Out in the field, it became a weapon against stubborn insects and enemies of the crop.

In space, nuclear energy powered satellites, both by compact reactors and by radioisotopic systems. These satellites performed such important duties as furnishing navigation information to sailors on the sea, both those in the Navy and those who ventured forth on their own.

The Atomic Energy Commission was discussing efforts with the U.S. Bureau of Mines and the Geological Survey on the use of underground nuclear explosions to fracture gold-bearing rocks. A leaching solution would then dissolve the gold, for pumping it to the surface. First considered in an experiment called Project Sloop for extracting copper, AEC scientists hoped to reduce the cost of gold production to less than $10 an ounce.

In the near future were such prospects as spaceships traveling in interplanetary space, propelled by small nuclear reactor systems. Their heating, cooling, air purification, lighting, instruments, and food preparation would be powered by nuclear energy as well.

Scientists dreamed of deserts turned into breadbaskets, with water made fresh and drinkable by nuclear plants which took the salt out of the sea. And on those seas, nuclear ships would move freely, harvesting food from the almost endless supply in the ocean.

And one day the nuclear attack submarine force, the nuclear ballistic missile submarine force, and the fledgling surface Navy would become a fully nuclear-powered Naval force capable of cruising anywhere in the world for indefinite lengths of time without the need for stopping in foreign ports.

But none of these developments would be possible without the doers, the innovators, the leaders, and yes, the pushers and gadflies if need be.

213

Admiral Hyman George Rickover felt strongly about the need for men who were not content to follow along with the crowd like so many sheep, for men who would express their opinions no matter how much they went against the prevailing tide. He was concerned about the intellectual climate which tended to discourage free and open discussion of divergent points of view.

"Independence of expression has now become almost unthinkable, yet an uncriticized society or institution will not endure. Only those who can express their opinions are free men. Unity is not unanimity," he said.

"The need for dissent and criticism is proclaimed within the Department of Defense, and dissent is what is lacking. In ways which officers themselves perceive only dimly or not at all, they are compromised or manipulated into conforming to the official 'line,' " he told a Congressional committee. His listeners smiled inwardly at the thought of anyone trying to compromise or manipulate Admiral Rickover.

Dissent is welcome, he pointed out, as long as it is irrelevant to the existing policies. When Rickover criticized American education, no one in the Pentagon was at all concerned, he said with a wry smile, because someone else was being criticized.

Fear of dissenting could lead to personal disaster, Rickover pointed out. As example, he related the story of General Wilhelm Keitel, who was Adolf Hitler's chief of the Combined General Staff. "Time after time, when he knew Hitler to be wrong, he failed to speak out, and so became one of the architects of German defeat," Rickover said.

"What proved fatal to Keitel was not his weaknesses, but his virtues—the virtues of a subordinate, a man with a mentality of a sergeant major, dressed up in a general's uniform. Duty, obedience, and loyalty were the code he clung to, by which he exercised all sense of responsibility. And, like patriotism, they were not enough. In a world like ours you cannot afford not to ask questions, or else you may end up as the leader of disaster," Rickover said.

"Keitel lived to sign Germany's unconditional surrender in 1945 and was subsequently hanged in accordance with sentence of the Nuremberg war crimes trial," he told the Congressional committee.

Then the admiral gave the other side of the picture, the case of the dissenter and the value of his dissent. The man's name was Admiral Charles Beresford of the British Navy.

"In 1887, as a captain assigned to the Admiralty, he strongly opposed the First Lord—the civilian head of the Admiralty—who was blocking a modernization shipbuilding program for the British fleet and attempting to suppress arguments by naval officers that the fleet was becoming outmoded and obsolete." The parallel between Rickover himself and the civilian hierarchy in the Defense Department did not escape the Congressmen.

"Captain Beresford proposed a fleet modernization and improvement program which was ignored by the civilian naval authorities. In January, 1888, Beresford resigned from the navy in protest against these actions of the First Lord's, and publicly campaigned in Parliament and in the press for the reforms he believed necessary. Three months later the First Lord recommended an identical program, and it was swiftly approved by Parliament.

"Captain Beresford was reappointed to active duty in 1889. In 1907, an admiral by then, he took command of the channel fleet when Lord Fisher was the senior naval officer at the Admiralty—the First Sea Lord. Admiral Beresford felt that the Admiralty's preparations for war were inadequate in that no general strategic plans had been prepared and the Admiralty had reorganized the home fleet into three separate divisions—at a time when Germany was concentrating her naval power in the North Sea.

"He complained publicly about this lack of preparation for war, even to the point of taking issue to the King, similar to what Admiral Sims of our own Navy did by going to President Theodore Roosevelt in 1906 when gunnery improvements were needed and the U.S. Navy would not adopt them. For this, Admiral Beresford was summarily retired by the Admiralty in 1909. But his proposed reforms were adopted: The British Naval War Staff was formed, and a single large fleet was established in home waters under a single commander. These measures he fought for were adopted barely in time to prepare the British Navy for the First World War and the Battle of Jutland.

"Would it not have been better for this dissent from within by a senior experienced officer to have been heeded and properly acted upon by the responsible authorities? Was the system a good one which on two occasions forced an outstanding officer to leave his service—forced him to air his views in public in order to achieve essential improvement in his service?"

In a sense, the question was one of Rickover's own career. Opposed by the Navy and by the civilians who controlled the Department of Defense, only Congress had managed to save his career time and time again. But, more important to him, it was Congress which had supported the program in which he believed so strongly. Without this one admiral and the Congressional committees who supported him, the nuclear Navy undoubtedly would have been many years delayed and probably never would have achieved so much initial success.

Rickover's own explanation of his actions was this: "I am attempting in whatever way I can to bring the Navy abreast of the world in which it lives; to face with intelligence the world of tomorrow. For if the Navy stands still, it will die.

"Some in the Navy are afraid of this new world that seems to have descended upon us so suddenly. For, as they see it, it is a world where the machine has replaced man, doubt has driven out certainty, when all the things we take for granted, that made life simple, are being questioned, turned inside out, subjected to 'radical revision.' It is not this new world that should be feared, but that we in the Navy say little or nothing that would justify our existence.

"We must not repeat yesterday's answers to tomorrow's problems, we must not retreat into the future.

We must not be talking to ourselves, because no one will listen or understand what we are saying."

Rickover also once summed up his own personal philosophy of dissent: "In some of my remarks I have expressed views that are contrary to the views of my superiors. As you are aware, there are basic differences in our opinions. I must make it clear that I claim no superior wisdom. Further, my superiors have responsibilities and problems that are different and more onerous than mine; those responsibilities and problems may require different solutions than I propose. I make no claim that my views are right and that others are wrong.

"I can only say what I know and what I believe. This is the only service I can perform for my country. . . .

"In my day-to-day life it would be easier for me not to voice my views, which are clearly controversial—not to speak out—not to 'rock the boat' or 'make waves'. . . . But in the serene life I would then lead I would soon find I couldn't live with myself. I believe each of us must make a personal decision: Are we to be concerned only with ourselves, or are we to be concerned with the welfare of our children and their children?

"Silence also is an act, an act of cowardice."

Bibliography

Anderson, William R., and Blair, Clay, Jr., *Nautilus 90° N* (Cleveland: World Publishing Co., 1959).

Baar, James, and Howard, William, *Polaris!* (New York: Harcourt, Brace & World, 1960).

Blair, Clay, Jr., *The Atomic Submarine and Admiral Rickover* (New York: Henry Holt, 1954).

Polmar, Norman, *Atomic Submarines* (Princeton, N.J.: Van Nostrand, 1963).

Rees, Ed, *The Seas and the Subs* (New York: Duell, Sloan and Pearce, 1961).

U.S. Naval History Division, *The Submarine in the U.S. Navy* (Washington: 1960).

Index

221

222

223

The Author

Heather M. David is Pentagon correspondent for Fairchild Publications, Inc., publishers of *Electronic News, Metalworking News, Daily News Record*, and several other trade newspapers and Fairchild Broadcast News. She formerly was with American Aviation Publications as editor of biotechnology and Capitol Hill correspondent. She is author of *Wernher von Braun*, another biography in Putnam's *Lives to Remember* series. She lives with her husband and their daughter, Laurel, in the Foggy Bottom section of Washington, D.C.